Economic Crisis

Explanation & Policy Options

Philip S. Salisbury

UNIVERSITY PRESS OF AMERICA,® INC.
Lanham • Boulder • New York • Toronto • Plymouth, UK

University Press of America,® Inc.
4501 Forbes Boulevard
Suite 200
Lanham, Maryland 20706
UPA Acquisitions Department (301) 459-3366

Unit A, Whitacre Mews, 26-34 Stannary Street,
London SE11 4AB, United Kingdom

Printed in the United States of America
British Library Cataloging in Publication Information Available

Library of Congress Control Number: 2015952130
ISBN: 978-0-7618-6683-1 (clothbound : alk. paper)
eISBN: 978-0-7618-6684-8

∞™ The paper used in this publication meets the minimum requirements of American National Standard for Information Sciences—Permanence of Paper for Printed Library Materials, ANSI Z39.48-1992

To Those Who Teach,
Whether in Life or in the Classroom

Beneath the surface there are unseen eddies
that determine the fate of economies

Contents

Tables and Figures

TABLES

FIGURES

Preface and Introduction

This book consists of a series of nine papers that address in some way the Great Recession, the economic conditions in the U.S., and estimates for total personal income or total personal disposable income.

The book presents some ground-breaking work in two areas. First, it provides a method for understanding business cycles. Economists have tried over the years to understand these complex phenomena with no success. Second, the foundation of the housing boom and bust was the level of effective demand. This boom and bust took place in an environment that forced its occurrence.

One of the primary purposes of the papers is to introduce a complex algorithm for estimating when business cycles have occurred.

Chapters 1–3 cover the estimation of personal income using Current Population Survey, Annual Social and Economic Supplement data. That data (from 2006), featured the population by ethnicity, sex, age group, and mean income. The data contained both population figures, and persons with income.

Chapter 4 covers the period of the Great Recession, first in a descriptive way, and then it seeks to estimate personal disposable income from 2000 through 2040. Estimated personal income (by method I) is used to historically estimate personal disposable income.

Chapter 6 sets forth an administrative and budgetary recognition of the need to give emphasis to the role of public-private partnerships in developing the U.S. alternative energy future.

Chapter 7 features an argument for the use of personal income in evaluating the larger economy. In particular the use of stress equations in which opposite sides of the equation create a balance or imbalance.

Chapter 8 provides additional detail that shows the variation in several quantities that support the link between economics and population.

The ends of Chapter 5 and the substance of Chapter 9 provide summary information and alternatives.

Chapter 10 addresses the Trans-Pacific Partnership (TPP), the deflation that is occurring in oil prices and their possible impact on the U.S. economy. Mixed inflation and deflation of the price of goods and services provides a mixed reaction by the private sector in passing price declines to consumers.

There may be some overlap in the chapters, as they were done independent of each other. The papers' coherence is in the theme that economics and population, at a detailed level are undeniably linked. The presence of any inadequacies or failings is that of the author alone.

CHAPTER 1

Implications for 2007 and Beyond

The economic circumstances in the United States now and during the 1929–1940 period have several elements in common. There were no bank failures in 2005 and 2006. There were three bank failures in 2007; there were 10 bank failures (to August 2008). The failure of Lehman Brothers on September 14, 2008, the decline of the Dow on September 16–17, 2008 by over 949 points, a housing crisis, a credit crisis, increasing unemployment, and declining confidence in the U.S. economy are factors that, although they are currently not as severe as the Great Depression, raise concerns about future potential decline.

Underlying the Great Depression Era were four dynamics. These dominant dynamics were variations in M_2 level, in bank reserves, in unemployment, and personal income. Secondly, the increase (1929–1933), decline (1937), and then increase (1938–1939) in the adjusted unemployment levels showed the evolving human impact of the Great Depression. Included in the number of unemployed is the population dynamic of the declining numbers of working age male immigrants. Over the period from 1930 to 1940 the decline was not being offset by equivalent numbers of immigrant, working age males. From 1931 through 1940, the annual number of immigrants was less than 100,000.

The period from 2007 to 2029 is affected by a different; though somewhat similar, dynamic; this dynamic is the aging of the 45–64 age and sex groups and these group's subsequent declining incomes. The purpose of this chapter is to demonstrate how the aging live birth data (See Figure 1.1) by age and sex group and application of mean income data can be used to roughly characterize the current and future effects of population subgroups on the U.S. economy.

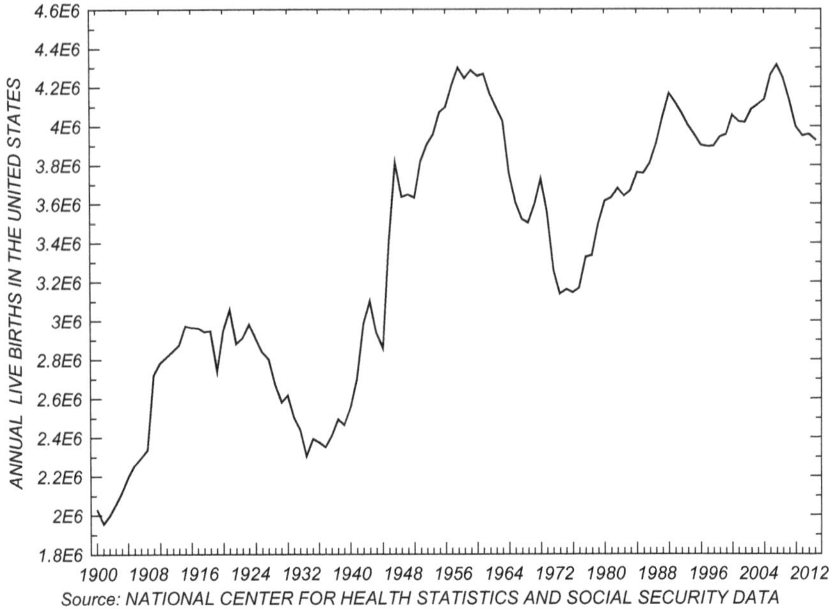

FIGURE 1.1: Annual Live Births in the U.S. 1900-2013

There was a continual growth in the number of live births in the U.S. between the low in 1933 and the peak from 1958–1960. This was an increase from 2.304 million live births in 1933 to 4.268 million in 1961. In the 1933 to 1961 period 97.488 million live births occurred. From there the annual number of live births declines from 4.268 million live births in 1961 to 3.144 million in 1975. That was a total of 54.54 million live births from 1961 to 1975.

In comparing these numbers, it becomes clear that the decrease in live births from 1961 to 1975 represents a major driver of the contraction of the economy. From a bottom of 3.144 million live births, in 1975, live births increased to 4.316 million live births in 2007. That means that 16 year olds will peak in 2023. All live birth numbers from 1976 to 2012 will exceed the low point in 1975. The decline in live births ion 2008–2012 is currently in process and will be repetitive although in a lesser degree of the decline from 1961 to 1975. This represents a significant demographic effect on personal income, personal consumption, and disposable personal income in the economy, especially as the live births reach maximum earnings age.

Why are these increases and decreases important? First, each year the number of surviving live births in a cohort ages. The number in the cohort declines. Secondly, when each year of live births reaches employable age, the earnings of the age group vary as the cohort ages. I will first examine the effect of live births aging. The number of live births from a given year can be multiplied by the survival rate of the cohort at a given age (see Box 1.1). This results in the number of individuals from a cohort remaining at given ages.

BOX 1.1

number surviving, t_0 to $t_{n.=}$

(Live births/year)(cohort survival values y_0 to y_n)

Second, only a portion of the persons surviving to a given age will participate in the labor force and be employed, or have a source of income. The labor force participation rate is used to determine the number in a population in the civilian labor force (CLF). The number in the CLF can be divided into three groups; those employed, those unemployed and searching for work, and those unemployed and not searching for work.

An illustration of this situation is provided in Figure 1.2. There are three principles to remember. First, if a year of live births is lagged a given number of years each datum of live births is the age of the lag. If a cohort is prepared from a year of live births and a survival curve, each data point on that curve

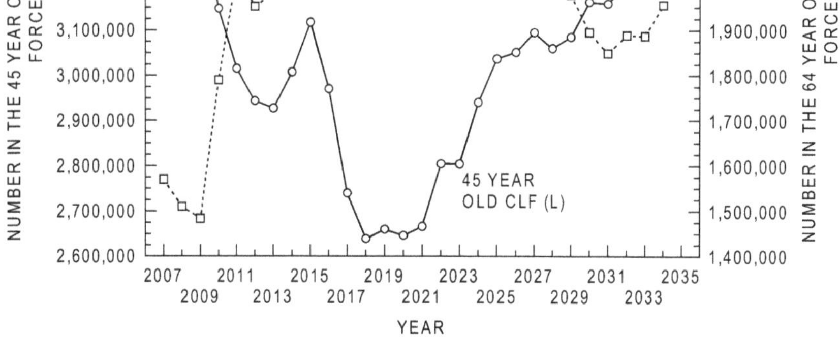

SOURCE: FROM LIVE BIRTH DATA (NCHS), SURVIVAL RATES (SOCIAL SECURITY) AND LABOR FORCE PARTICIPATION RATES (BUREAU OF LABOR STATISTICS)

FIGURE 1.2: Civilian Labor Force 45 Years Old Compared to the Civilian Labor Force 64 Years old, 2007-2024

represents the number surviving at that time. Figure 1.2 characterizes surviving live births lagged 45 years in the civilian labor force and surviving live births lagged 64 years in the civilian labor force versus the year in which the lagged data point occurs.

What is of note about Figure 1.2? Between the 45-year-old civilian labor force line and the 64-year-old civilian labor force line there are lags of 46, 47, 48, 49, 50, 51, 52, 53, 54, 55, 56, 57, 58, 59, 60, 61, 62, and 63 years which are not shown. Thus, the lagged 45 and 64 year old lines are only being used to represent all those lines between 45 and 64. In the year 2006 and beyond to 2018–2021 the number of individuals declines to a four year trough. Where are the 45–64-year olds going? They are aging as well as dying. The number of individuals becoming 64 grows and then declines.

Every lag of live births, from 45 to 64, needs to be multiplied by the survival rate for a given year and a given age level's sex. The surviving 45–64-year olds have been multiplied by their survival rates. Second, each line of lagged live births is multiplied by its labor force participation rate to result in the number in the civilian labor force. What conclusions can we draw from this graph (Figure 1.2) and supporting data in Table 1.1?

Figure 1.2 shows the decline in the civilian labor force (CLF) for a 45-year lag compared to the rise in the 64-year-old CLF (2007–2034). The correlation between the two CLF lines is r= -.76 (N=28, p=0.000). The total in the 45-year-old CLF line from 2007 to 2034 is 84.89 million persons. The overall number in the 45-year-old CLF from 2007 to 2021 is 44.79 million individuals.

Continuing the analysis of Figure 1.2, from 2007 to 2021, the 45-year-old CLF declines a sum of 44.79 million persons. From 2022 to 2030, the 45-year-old CLF increases by a sum of 27.05 million persons. The sixty-four year old CLF increased by a sum of 38.51 million persons from 2007 to 2025. From 2007 through 2033, 54.50 million 64 year old CLF persons became 65 years or older. This figure represents approximately 17.35 percent of the current U.S. population. From 2011 to 2029, 64-year-olds outnumber 45-year-olds by 14.61 million individuals. Figure 1.2 shows the decline in the CLF for 45-year-olds. There is a roughly reciprocal incline in the number of live births in the 64-year lag from 2015–2021. Thus, the departure of these people from income-receiving status will have a major impact on the economy. This can be explained by two major factors. First, the decline in the absolute numbers in the 45-year-old lagged live births (really 45–54-year-old females and older) means that there will be fewer income receivers at those ages. The peak and then declining incomes of males 55–64 old and above have a significant impact on the U.S. economy.

TABLE 1.1. Number of Males and Females With Income by Age Category and Mean Income: 2006*

Age Category	Number of Males (000)	Mean Income per Person	Total Male Income (Billions)	Number of Females (000)	Mean Income per Person	Total Female Income (Billions)
15-24	14,093	$15,213	$214.397	13,267	$12,290	$163.051
25-34	19,045	32,131	611.935	17,151	29,693	509.265
35-44	20,374	42,637	868.686	19,199	34,762	667.396
45-54	20,247	45,693	925.147	20,135	36,740	739.730
55-64	14,905	57,219	852.849	15,073	33,289	501.765
65-74	8,417	39,435	335.868	9,781	21,588	211.152
75 & over	6,547	30,623	199.750	9,975	17,990	179.450

*Current Population Survey, Annual Social and Economic Supplement (ASEC), U.S. Census Bureau, http://pubdb3.census.gov/macro/032007/perinc/new01_019.htm, Accessed March 23, 2008, 2006 Income data is from 2007 Current Population Survey, ASEC

These tables and figures give us the evidence from which to draw conclusions about the current dynamics of population and income. First, Table 1.1 and Figure 1.3, derived from Table 1.1 demonstrates how mean income differs for different age and sex groups. Based on what Table 1.1, Figure 1.2, Figure 1.3, and Figure 1.4 reveal, the following observations can be made:

- Male income increases from a mean of 15,213 dollars for the 15–24 age category to a maximum of a mean of 57,219 dollars for the 55–64 age group. Average incomes decline from that peak to an average of 30,623 dollars for those 75 and above (2006 current dollars).
- Female mean income increases from a low of 12,290 dollars for the 15–24 year age category, to a peak of 36,740 dollars for 45–54-year-olds. Mean income declines from that peak to 30,623 dollars for those 75 years and older (2006 current dollars).
- In Figure 1.2 the lagged CLF line for 45 year old starts declining from 2007. The decline plateaus in 2018–2021 and begins a gradual increase from 2022 to 2024.
- When interpreted, Figure 1.2 means that the 45–54 female year old group and the 55–64 year old group are aging. These are respectively the two highest average income groups for both females and males. These age and sex categories are aging and total incomes will decline accordingly.
- The decline in the number of individuals in the four groups, with the average incomes as they age from 64 years to 65 years and older, will persist

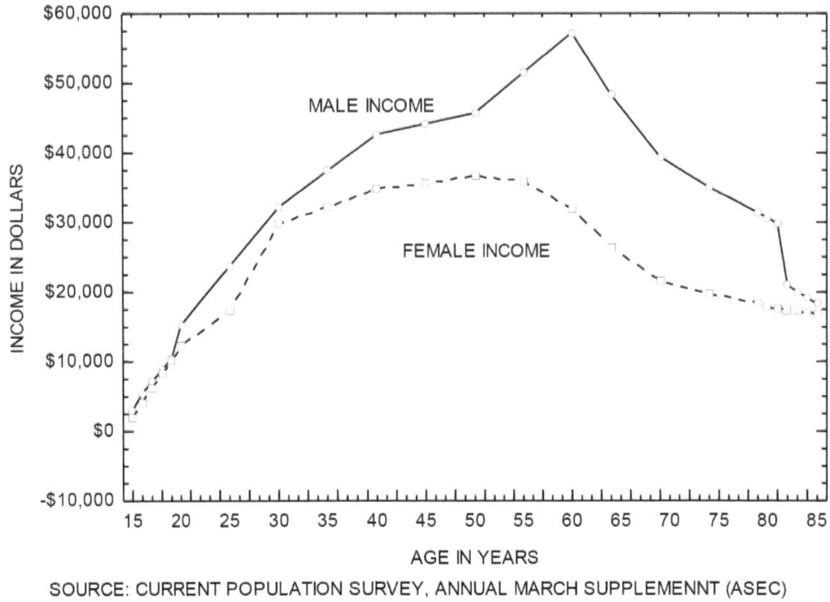

FIGURE 1.3: Distribution of Male and Female Income, Ages 15–85, 2006

from 2008–2021 and likely beyond. This 14-year period will bring slowly increasing total personal income. In summary, the five weeks (September 7 through October 14, 2008) witnessed collapsing financial institutions (Bear Sterns, Fannie Mae, Freddie Mac, and AIG, Washington Mutual Inc), and the adoption of a rescue package. In one week the stock market (Dow) dropped about 1,580 points. There will continue to be more volatility and downturns. Several important conclusions can be drawn.

- Personal income in the United States is increasing at a decreasing rate. Unemployment may increase gradually. Even with appropriate policies, the depression may only be moderated.
- It is clear that this is both a housing crisis and a credit crisis. The source of the housing crisis was that housing was overbuilt. In other terms, the number of individuals at house purchasing age has been in decline and will continue to decline. Of all homebuyers, 34 percent are ages 45–64 (National Association of Realtors, 2007). The credit crisis has occurred because of all the bad mortgages and loans written. Bundling of mortgages, creating securities out of them, and insuring the securities when the sources of the securities cannot be traced created a hazard for banks and the stock market.

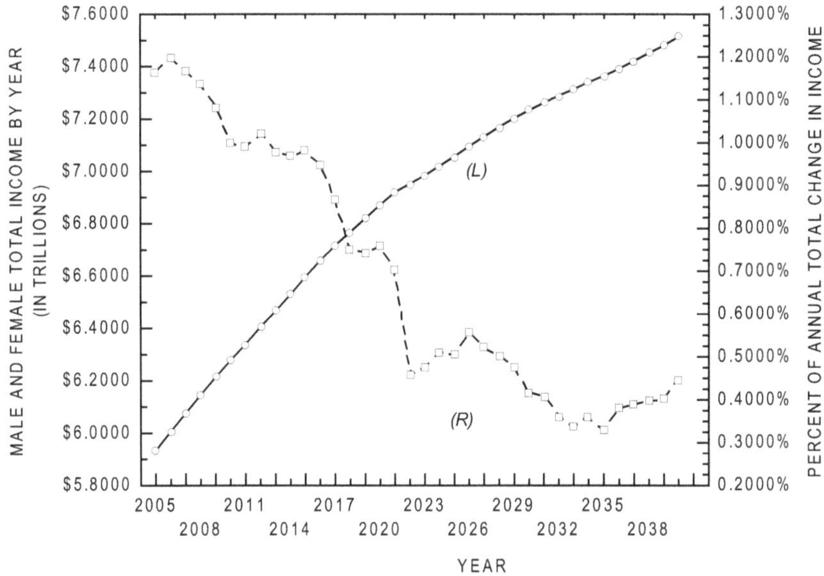

SOURCE: 2007 CURRENT POPULATION SURVEY (CPS), ASEC, AND ESTIMATED POPULATION BY AGE GROUP AND SEX (U.S. CENSUS BUREAU), 2005 - 2040

FIGURE 1.4: Estimated Male and Female Total Personal Income by Year and Percent Change per Year 2005–2040

- Banks became reluctant to loan money to others because of a lack of confidence in the borrower's ability to repay.
- As the number of people 45 and over declines, assets will be used in retirement, and pension funds will decline in value.
- In these circumstances, the numbers of people in certain age groups will decline. Under these conditions of declining age group numbers, and declining incomes, total personal income, disposable personal income, and total disposable personal income will increase at a decreasing rate.
- The surviving live births lagged 45 years from 1984 to 2029 will age out of the 45-year-old lag category and eventually the 64-year-old lag category. This estimated level of change in the CLF for those respective ages will affect the actual number of individuals, male and female surviving to the dates on the X axis of Figure 1.2. By applying survival rate, labor force participation rates, and unemployment rates more accurate numbers are obtained. An alternative method is to use Census data for populations of age and sex categories, multiply each by their respective personal income

participation rate (PIPR), and multiply that by the mean income for the sex and age groups (see Figure 1.3, personal income line).
- Employing those out of work in productive employment to the point that immigration is needed should be a policy goal. This would preferably be done with in-country clean-energy projects.
- Figure 1.4 shows that total personal income will increase at a decreasing rate from 2005–2040.
- The periods from 2015–2019, 2020–2021, and 2022–2040 will be periods of significant economic turmoil in the U.S. Chapters VI and Chapter IX offer some alternatives for government, and government-private action.

In summary, this analysis deals primarily with the population effects from 2000–2040. Government assistance as a last resort has come into play. The mating habits of U.S. citizens are subject to the influences of history. The likelihood that we cannot control levels of live births leaves us at the mercy of these powerful demographic forces. The U.S. economy faces a major problem due to the lack of effective demand (Keynes 1936) and the relocation of jobs overseas. Resources used by the government need to be directed at these problems in cooperation with the private-sector.

The major trends that will impact the U.S. economy are (1) the trend lower in numbers of higher wage earning and higher income age, sex, and ethnicity groups. (2) The increasing number of older (greater than 65 years old) persons with income. (3) Groups in (2) will have decreased income. (4) As of 2020–2021 forward there will be major trends contradicting each other. From 2021 on there will be an increase in those in the greater income groups (45–49 years), and (50–55 years). This trend will be countered by the growing group of those 65 plus years of age and having lower incomes. The exact form the resolution of these countervailing trends will be seen. It will be a period of recovery in the U.S. economy.

CHAPTER 2

Live Births, Population, and Economic Impact

The research in this chapter investigates John Maynard Keynes' (1937) hypothesis that population declines affect consumption. This chapter explores this hypothesis by examining males and females with income 45–64 years of age. Live birth data from 1900 to 2011 (NCHS 1909–2011, Social Security 1900–1908) are used with Social Security decennial survival data to create annual survival tables from 1900 to 2020. The effect of survival rates of different age groups is demonstrated. It is concluded that declines in the number of persons in the 45–64 age categories will result in a declining rate of increase in personal income and disposable personal income in the 2007–2019 period and perhaps further out.

HYPOTHESIS AND BACKGROUND

The hypothetical effects of population changes were discussed by Keynes (1937). Keynes had no data to justify the case he made for a decline in consumption with a decline in population. This chapter will confirm the hypothesis that live births (see Figure 2.1) have an important, lagged, impact on the U.S. economy. Furthermore, the impact of live births is moderated by their survival rate, sex, income and ethnicity.

Malthus's (1798, 1993) model set forth a dynamic growth process. As nations grow in wealth these nations approach a steady per capita income. Death rates decline and fertility increases. The experience in developing nations in the twentieth century has been that fertility declined as incomes rose. It is the effects of population decline that this chapter will address.

Reddaway (1939) maintained in examining the changes in demand for particular products, declining population makes a very big difference. It may be the instance that a relatively insignificant decline for one commodity resulted in no identifiable disturbance. The general rise in consumption may mask the smaller decline in the consumption of a single commodity. In the case of population decline a danger of over-capacity exists. Reddaway (1939) concludes that population decline will increase the adjustment that is necessary and reduce the ability of the economic system to respond smoothly. Reddaway (1939) does not support any of his theorizing with empirical evidence.

It is the effects of population decline that have occasionally been addressed since Keynes'work (1937). Joan Robinson (1951) addressed the effects of population decline. During World War II she wrote a chapter in anticipation of a declining population in Great Britain following the war. She argues that a decline in population would likely have the result of either curtailing booms or deepening or extending declines. In those circumstances, the risk to industry would reduce incentives to invest. Robinson (1951) wrote that with a stable or declining population, full employment would lead to a rising standard of living, although she remained open to what form a rising standard of living might take. She (1951) further observes that the age composition of the population rather than its total numbers is most relevant to employment trends.

The United Nations (Population Division, 1953) concludes that population changes tend to affect the pattern as well as the volume of consumption. It is suggested that the empirical studies on the effect of population on patterns and aggregate of consumption are scattered and fragmentary. As such, these studies do not allow generalizations to be made for all economies. Some of the complicating conditions have to do with the inter-relationships of demographic factors with social and economic factors. The chapter suggests that consumption links population changes to economic changes which subsequently, through consumption, affect population changes. To better understand this dynamic process of consumption, economic and population characteristics it is suggested that the information on these topics needs to be summarized, integrated and supplemented by new studies.

Denton and Spencer (1975) develop age productivity profiles for Canadian males and females using 1951 and 1961 census data. The productivity weight for a given sex's cohort depends on both the year it was born and its age. Upon reaching working age a cohort experiences proportional changes in productivity as it grows older. A questionable assumption is that these productivity changes are the same for all cohorts. Denton and Spencer (1975) develop a ten parameter economic-demographic model to simulate the effects of exogenous changes in the total fertility rate and the rate of net immigration. Their chapter (1973) and book (1975) explore other economic-demographic models for use in simulation studies. Denton and Spencer (1975) admit that the developed models relate to no existing economy or population. They do suggest that the *simulation-theoretic* models are very powerful.

In a subsequent chapter (Denton and Spencer, 1976), develop a consumption function that uses demographic, household, and population effects. They develop an approach that starts at the microeconomic level and proceeds to the macroeconomic level. Their consumption function provides for a lifetime pattern of consuming and savings that reflects changes in household situations over time. One of the results of their research using Canadian data was that consumption was not affected by average household size or the age distribution of the population. This chapter takes a different approach and empirically documents that the number in defined sex and age groups will decline over time and suggests that this decline in numbers of individuals of working age affects total income. The chapter uses age and sex as control variables and suggests that further refinements of demographics are possible to understand how they affect income.

This chapter differs in that it is data-based and makes an effort to make accurate annual estimates of selected male and female age group populations in the United States for the 2007–2040 period. In doing so, it distinguishes between different annual levels of live births (for males and females), those having different proportions of each group with income, those with different mean incomes, and those with different annual survival rates.

Kuznets (1973) maintains that 71 percent of GNP is allocated to private, individual consumer consumption. This includes 6 percent of government expenditures that are devoted to direct services to consumers. In stating the aggregate form of total demand the role of the individual is noted on the consumption side of the equation. Personal income is a constraint on personal consumption. The disaggregation of personal income may be taken to the subgroup level (see Box 2.1).

$$PI = \sum_{x=1}^{x=m}(N_{xt}\,\overline{pi}_{xt}) \qquad (2.1)$$

The terms are defined as follows:

PI = aggregate personal income

N_{xt} = number in subgroup x (x = 1...m) at or during time t

$\overline{pi}_{xt}$ = average personal income of subgroup x at or during time t

This chapter does not delve into factors that affect personal income other than age and sex. Additional candidate variables are education (Schultz 1963, and Becker 1993), marital status, and ethnicity. The relationship of sex, age, education, ethnicity, and income has been adequately illustrated in *American Incomes, Demographics of Who has Money* (2007). Income in 2005 peaks in the 45 through 54 age category for both males and females with income. These facts, in particular, are relevant to the presentation and analysis presented in this chapter (see note 1 at end of chapter).

PART I

The History of Live Births and the Use of Live Birth Lags

Figure 2.1, the history of live births in the United States (U.S.) from 1909 – 2013, demonstrates that over that period there has been a great deal of variation in live birth numbers. Periods of decline in live births were for 1914–1917, 1918–1919, 1921–1922, 1924–1929, 1930–1933, 1934–1936, 1938–1939, and 1943–1945. The low point of annual live births in the Depression Era in the U.S. was 1933 (2,304,000). The high point for annual live births was in 1957

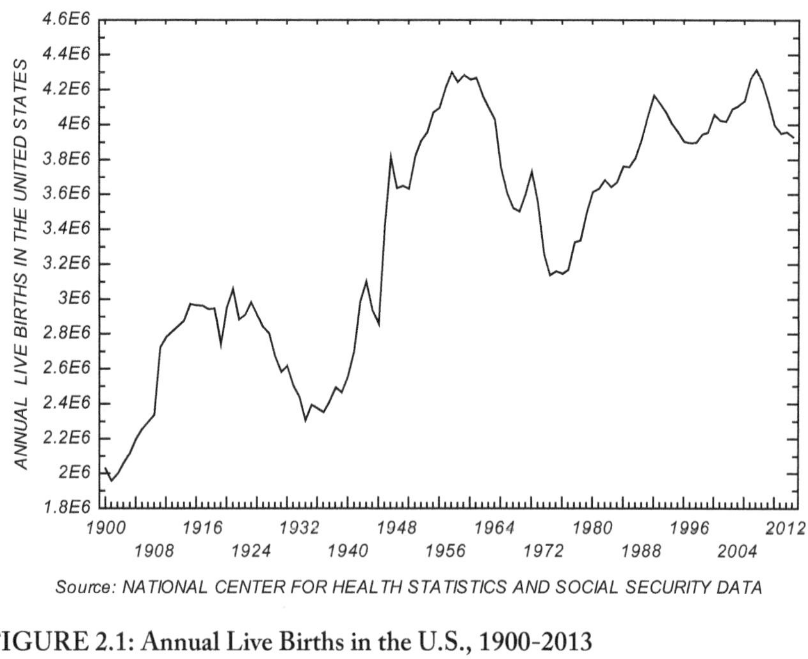

FIGURE 2.1: Annual Live Births in the U.S., 1900-2013

(4,300,000). A secondary peak occurs in 1991 followed by a trough 1997. Then, live births in the U.S. increase, decrease, and increase again to 2006.

To understand some of the economic impact of the demographics, annual live births were lagged forward 45 years while adjusting for the survival rate of males and females above 45 years of age.

Similarly, the live births for males and females were lagged 74 years and multiplied by their respective survival rates (see Figure 2.2).

Additionally, the survivors were multiplied by the personal income participation rate (PIPR) (the proportion of the surviving population with income). These data are displayed in Figure 2.3. It is important to note that Figures 2.1, 2.2, and 2.3 are static. Figure 2.3 lags the 1909 live births 48 years forward (that is, it ages live births by lagging them 48 years forward and adjusting them for their survival rate and PIPR). This can be compared to live births with a lag of 74 years adjusted for their survival rate and PIPR. If live births are lagged 48 years, all live birth points (adjusted for survival rate and PIPR) are 48 years of age. If adjusted live births are lagged 74 years and multiplied by their PIPR, all live birth points are 74 years of age (see Figure 2.1). That is, the live birth graphic is static. All the live births for a given year after adjustment for the survival rate for the sex and year of live births will represent the expected persons surviving at that number of the years lagged. Multiplication by the appropriate PIPR yields the respective numbers of each age level who have income.

Figure 2.2 and Figure 2.3 are also important because they demonstrate that the large increase in live births adjusted for the survival rate or those with income is moving to the right on the figure as it ages. This aging of the adjusted live birth population and its associated incomes affect total income in the U.S. economy. There will be a significant decrease in the rate of change in total personal income for specific age groups spanning the approximate period of 2016–2038. This 22 year period will be the period it takes for the baby boom generation to pass partially through the U.S. economy.

According to *American Incomes, Demographics of Who Has Money* (Editors of New Strategist Publications, 2007) incomes fell for most household sizes between 2000 and 2005 (p. 24). This decline is a harbinger of things to come.

Over the 48 year interval from 1909 to 1957 the cohort of live births starting out at 2,718,000 live births in 1909 declines to 2,546,929 in 1957. The number surviving at 72 years old will be 1,879,116 persons (.69136 x 2,718,000), a decline of 838,884 persons. Not included in this is the decline in total personal income for that age group due to (1) death, and (2) declining incomes with increasing age beyond the 45–54 year age level. Table 2.2 will present an estimate of the number surviving for those aged 48 years as they age to 74 years.

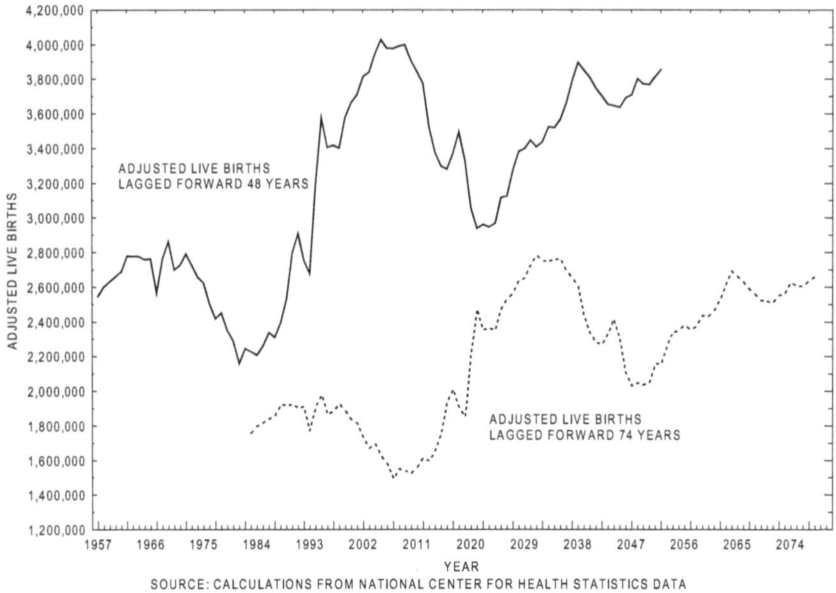

FIGURE 2.2: Adjusted Live Births Lagged 48 and 74 Years

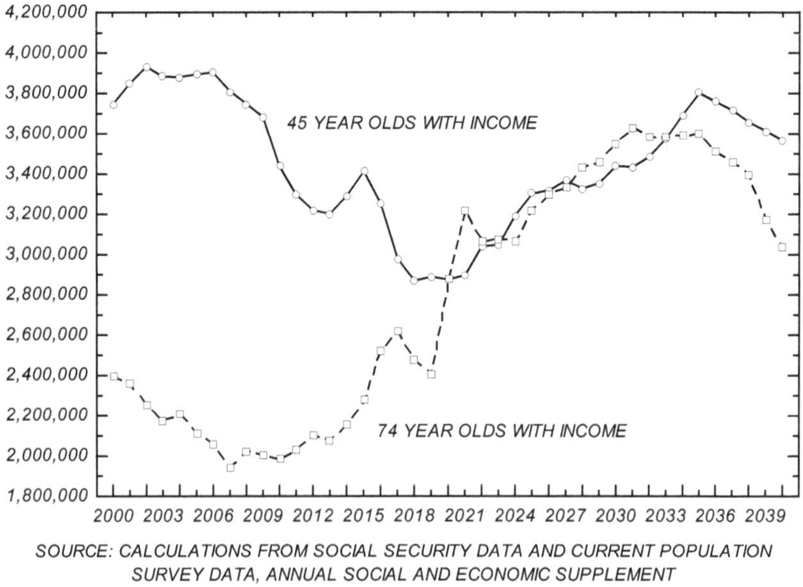

FIGURE 2.3: Males and Females with Income 45 years old and 75 Years Old

Figure 2.1 provides a hint at the complexity of what is occurring. For every cohort of 48 year olds that comes into being there is a similar, annual, recurring process. Figure 2.4 provides a portrayal of the decline in the number of individuals 48 years of age in 1948, the numbers that survive, and the cumulative number deceased in that group from 48 years of age to depletion of the cohort.

Figure 2.3 reveals that each data point along the lagged live birth line that has been lagged 48 years represents those live births surviving to that year. Similarly, each data point along the lagged live birth line that has been lagged 74 years represents those live births surviving to that year. Figure 2.3 compares adjusted live births lagged forward 48 years to adjusted live births lagged 74 years forward.

When all the groups of those aged 48 years and older are treated similarly, with their respective survival rates, an additive effect develops. Each successive group of 48 year olds has its own survival curve starting at the cohort's birth year. Since the survival curve does nothing but decline (see Figure 2.4), the combined impact for these groups of 48 year olds (depending on their beginning numbers, and their survival rate) is to decline in numbers as they age. Figure 2.4 provides an example of how the beginning number of persons lagged 48 years and adjusted for survival, lives out its life as a cohort.

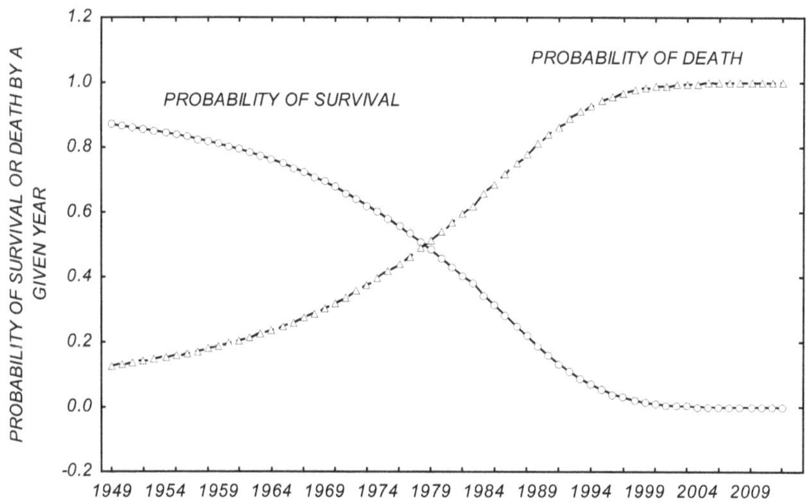

Source: Social Security and National Center for Health Statistics Data

FIGURE 2.4: Number Surviving and Cumulative Number Deceased from Initial Cohort of 1948 Live Births, 48 Years Old and Older

Figure 2.4 demonstrates the attrition of the living 48 year old cohort and the cumulative number of deceased. With significantly large numbers, the survival curves and cumulative death curves are marked by their regularity of decline and increase respectively as their cohort ages.

CONCLUSION: APPROXIMATELY 2007 AND THEREAFTER

Table 2.1 is used to calculate a rough estimate of the possible loss in income between those 48 years of age in 2007 as men and women arrive at the year 2040 (a change of 33 years).

Table 2.1 allows a determination of the effect of the passage of the baby boomers as they proceed through their maximum earning years. It is again emphasized that all points on the 48 year lag represent those who are 48 years old and all points on the 74 year lag represent those who are 74 years old. The period of particular difficulty will be 2015–2016 through 2021. The years used for comparison were 2007 and intermittent years through 2040. The incomes for 2008 (Current Population Survey, ASEC, 2009) are used as annual incomes for calculations of total personal income for a given age group and year.

What is of significance economically is that the large live birth increase which developed in the 1933–1960 period is passing through its maximum earning years. As it does so, this will translate into declining mean income,

TABLE 2.1: Number of Males and Females With Income by Age Category and Mean Income: 2006*

Age Category	Number of Males (000)	Mean Income per Person	Total Male Income (Billions)	Number of Females (000)	Mean Income per Person	Total Female Income (Billions)
15-24	14,093	$15,213	$214.397	13,267	$12,290	$163.051
25-34	19,045	32,131	611.935	17,151	29,693	509.265
35-44	20,374	42,637	868.686	19,199	34,762	667.396
45-54	20,247	45,693	925.147	20,135	36,740	739.730
55-64	14,905	57,219	852.849	15,073	33,289	501.765
65-74	8,417	39,435	335.868	9,781	21,588	211.152
75 & over	6,547	30,623	199.750	9,975	17,990	179.450

*Current Population Survey, Annual Social and Economic Supplement (ASEC), U.S. Census Bureau, http://pubdb3.census.gov/macro/032007/perinc/new01_019.htm, Accessed March 23, 2008, 2006 Income data is from 2007 Current Population Survey, ASEC.

and therefore, total income for the 45 – 64 age groups as these cohorts age. This will be due to two primary causes: (1) the numbers in these age categories will decline; and (2) their mean income will decline. In the approximate twenty-four years following the 48 year lag, adjusted live births decline from an adjusted 3,977,628 persons in 2007 to an adjusted 1,643,363 persons in 2032. That represents a decline of 2,334,265 persons. Importantly, this is for only one year of live birth data. This translates into an approximate decline in men's mean income from 62,294 dollars (in 2006) to approximately 35,431 dollars (in 2007, U.S. Census Bureau, Current Population Survey, Annual Social and Economic Supplement). The decline in women's mean income is estimated to be from 34,762 dollars (in 2006) to approximately 13,302 dollars (in 2032) (U.S. Census, Current Population Survey, Annual Social and Economic Supplement, Bureau 2007). This represents a decline in women's mean income of 26,237 dollars and assumes incomes to remain constant at 2006 levels. The estimated decline in income between the cohort of all lagged 48 years at the year 2007 to the year at which the lag is 72 years (2032) (a 72 year lag from the initial live birth year) is 113.48 billion dollars annually. This does not count the mean income and decline for other cohorts of age-income-receiving persons in each of the years between 2007 and 2040.

In summary of Part I, it is clear that an important decrease in income between the selected years, and therefore consumption, will occur given the conditions described in this chapter. The overall situation foreshadows the U.S. economy experiencing recession-like conditions for an extended period. Policymakers will be confronted with some daunting demographic and economic circumstances. These Figures and Tables present data supporting Keynes's hypothesis that population can influence economic prosperity. Keynes' hypothesis is modified to take into consideration the survival rate of each cohort, the personal income participation rate (PIPR), and the mean income of each cohort controlling for sex, and age.

PART II

Purpose, Data, and Methodology

To strengthen this summary, an empirical analysis was conducted to demonstrate what would happen from 2007 to 2019 to male and female populations 45–54 years of age and those 35–44 years of age, both having income.

The purpose of Part II is to put forth a method for estimating population in the United States 2007 (U.S.) in four ten-year sex and age groups and set forth the results of these estimates. The groups for which the working populations will be estimated are males 45–54 years of age, females 45–54 years of age, males 35–44 years of age, and females 35–44 years of age. The following data were used in the calculations:

- Live birth data from 1900 to 1908 (Social Security) and 1909 to 2004 (National Center for Health Statistics) were used.
- Decennial survival tables (decimal fraction surviving) used by Social Security (1900– 2100) were data entered.
- Proportion of newborn males (.51176) and newborn females (.48824) born each year were calculated. These proportions were estimates from an average of 20 years of male and of 20 years of female live birth data.

The steps in calculations of aggregate personal income and group personal income appear in Boxes 2.1 through 2.4.

$$PI = \sum_{x=1}^{x=m}(N_{xt}\,\overline{pi}_{xt}) \qquad (2.1a)$$

The terms are defined as follows:

PI = aggregate personal income

N_{xt} = number in subgroup x (x = 1...m) at or during time t

$\overline{pi}_{xt}$ = average personal income of subgroup x at or during time t

1. Total live births (TLB) for each year (1900–2020) were multiplied by the proportion expected to be males (.51176) and the proportion expected to be females (.48824). This resulted in the number of male live births and the number of female live births in a given year (Y or time t).

$$((TLB_t)^*(.51176)) = MLB_t \qquad (2.2)$$

$$((TLB_t)^*(.48824)) = FLB_t \qquad (2.3)$$

MLB_t= Male live births at or during time t

FLB_t= Female live births at or during time t

2. From 1900 through 1939 the first 13 years (rows) of survivors for both males and females were deleted. From 1940 on to the year 2020 the first 15 years (rows) of data were deleted. This was done to eliminate those not of working age.

3. Starting with year 1901, the survivors were lagged forward the number of years consistent with the year number of the live births after 1900. This created a lower triangular matrix. The lower triangular matrix was zero-filled to create a rectangular matrix.

4. The number of male or female live births was multiplied by the year of their survival rates for males and females respectively to get NS_{MT} or NS_{FT}.

5. Step seven (4) yielded the number of males or females of a given birth cohort surviving to a given age.

6. Using another, but different approach, annual live births may be lagged a specified number of years (Y_N). Each year of the annual lagged live births (Y) are the age of their lag (N).

7. To obtain the number surviving to that age the survival values (PS $_M$ or $_F$) of the sex and age (N) are multiplied times the lag values of live births (Y).

$$(Y_N)(PS_{N\,(M\text{ or }F)}) =$$

Survival vector of all males or females a given age (N).

$$= V_{M,S} \text{ or } V_{F,S}$$

8. To obtain the number in a given lag who have personal income (N_{PI}) the value of N is multiplied by the personal income participation rate (PIPR) (the proportion of persons that sex and age who have income).

$$N_{PI} = (PIPR_{(M\text{ or }F),\,S})(V_{(M\text{ or }F),\,S})$$

9. To get the total personal income for a given lag:

$$(N_{PIt})(\overline{PI}_t) = TOTPI_t \qquad (2.4)$$

PI = personal income, $\overline{PI}$ = average personal income

$TOTPI_t$ = total personal income at time t

RESULTS

What do these estimates indicate is likely to happen? Figure 2.5 indicates there will be an impact on income from the decline in males and females 45 years of age with income during the 2007–2021 period. Males and females 74 years old with income decrease in numbers during the 2015–2021 period. The aging of individuals from 65 to 74 years and above means declining incomes for them.

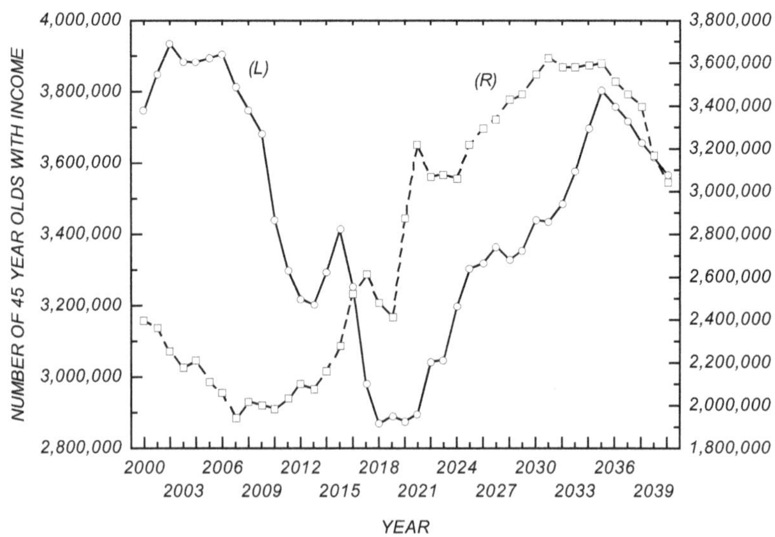

SOURCE: CALCULATIONS FROM SOCIAL SECURITY DATA AND CURRENT POPULATION SURVEY, ANNUAL SOCIAL AND ECONOMIC SUPPLEMENT DATA

FIGURE 2.5: Males and Females with Income, 45 Year Olds and 74 Year Olds

The data calculations resulted in the following one figure that provides data traces on annual male total income, annual female total income, total personal income, and the annual rate of change in total personal income (see Figure 2.6).

The two population groups (males 16–65+ and females 16–65+) show very different patterns of total income change. In Figure 2.6, the male, female, and *combined* populations, with income appear to increase at a steady rate. Visual inspection is deceiving. When total income is separated into its male and female components, and the annual rate of change for the income of each group is calculated and summed, both groups are increasing in personal income at a decreasing rate. This view is strengthened when the annual percent change in total personal income is calculated (see Figure 2.6). In fact, total personal income is increasing at a decreasing rate. The decline from 2015 to 2023 is dramatic. Figure 2.6 forebodes of a period of severe economic stress for the U.S. economy.

Caution must be taken in interpreting these population numbers because increases in productivity may nullify the losses in income due to population change. A complex dynamic is set up in which a decline in demand may build inventories thus allowing industry some relief from pressures to improve productivity. The record for three types of productivity in the 1995 through

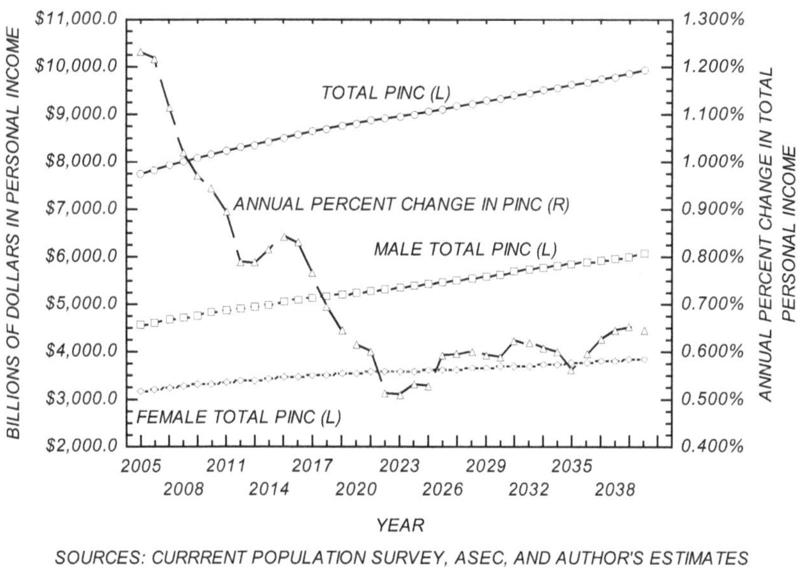

FIGURE 2.6: Total Personal Income, Male Personal Income, Female Personal Income, and Percent Annual Change in Total Personal Income, in 2008 dollars

2006 period showed the following: manufacturing productivity experienced a range of annual change from 1.6 percent to 6.9 percent; business productivity experienced a range of annual change from .1 percent to 4.1 percent; and, non-farm business experienced a range of annual change from .5 percent to 4.1 percent (Bureau of Labor Statistics 2007).

A second caveat needs to be made concerning the level of exports to U.S. trading partners. High demand for U.S. exports in tandem with a lower value of the dollar could stimulate production of goods and offset declines in demand in the U.S.

Third, government capital expenditures may be adjusted through the budgetary process.

This and gross domestic capital investment are unpredictable quantities in an environment of declining population sex and age groups.

Fourth, high energy prices, the mortgage crisis, a decline in housing starts, an overbuilt real estate market, the credit crunch (in which households in the United States have accumulated approximately 10,000 dollars of credit apiece (Truth About Credit, 2008)), job out-sourcing, inflationary trends in staples like food and gas, and a volatile stock market all make the economy uncertain.

Last, a recent development has been foreign investment in United States' businesses that are in financial difficulties. Oil producing nations, in particular, have accumulated significant amounts of money and are now investing it in the U.S. It remains to be seen if this will ameliorate the impact of declining population or declining total income in specified age groups.

CHAPTER 3

Demography and Economic Change

The relationship of several conditions to population and economics, and economic growth in particular, has been a challenge to economists and demographers alike. In an early book of lectures) on economic growth Simon Kuznets (1959) defined the unit of analysis as the nation-state. In doing so, he was aware of major distinctions between nation-states. For example, there may be differences in resources and in their quantity and quality. Such differences included population, ethnicities, land mass, weather, human capital, mean and per capita income, and in the nation-state's ability to adapt to new technology to name a few. However, it has been very difficult to determine the differences between the social, technological, and the economic aspects of nation-states (Kuznets 1973). This study presents a set of complex conditions for analysis and discussion.

Other conditions contribute to economic growth and decline. Innovation (in terms of nature and rates), competition, redundancy, the stage of economic development, the size of inventories, the qualitative and quantitative nature of demand (Kuznets 1959), efficiency, profits, product costs, labor costs, the structure of industry, and unpaid family labor are all contributing factors. In industrialized countries the movement from an agricultural-based economy to an industrialized economy and then to a modern economy constitutes economic growth.

Kuznets (1965) stated the case for population growth when the crude birth rate exceeds the crude death rate plus net immigration. Kuznets (1965) further suggested that population growth preceded growth in per capita income and that a decline in the death rate may affect economic growth. He suggested that stages of economic growth should be studied. Furthermore, he discussed the allocation of income from industrial sectors to income streams, to allocation of income, and to capital allocation.

One consideration that needs to be addressed in writing on economic growth is the dependency ratio. The dependency ratio signifies the ability of an economy to support persons under 15 and over 64 years of age who are unemployed and rely on the remainder of the population (15–64 years) to support them. This can be disaggregated into a child dependency ratio (0–14/15–64) and an aged dependency ratio (65 and over/15–64). A high dependency ratio means that a society or nation-state is relying on a smaller number of individuals to financially support the dependent population.

Change in industrial sectors results in changing income streams that fund the productive factors of enterprise, labor, and property. Industrial sectors act as both the originators and distributors of income and capital. Kuznets (1965) identifies the distribution of income payments to recipients categorized by income size or defined social groups. Income is distributed between capital formation and consumption. Goods and services become differentiated between those developed domestically and those involved in the import and export trade. These factors need to be addressed when studying in both the quantitative and the qualitative aspects of economic growth. The paucity of data limits the types of analysis that can be performed.

Kuznets (1966) defined economic growth in terms of a continuous increase in the population with a steady or growing per capita product. The author prefers an alternative to the use of per capita product. Per capita product is a ratio of total product to the total population. Using per capita product mistakenly spreads product across individuals who have no income or produce no product, thus diluting the product rather than attribute the product to those producing it. As was shown earlier, mean personal income per group multiplied by the number of persons in the group receiving income can be used to estimate total group income as well as total personal income. Mean income per group of those receiving income will be used.

Kuznets (1966) maintains that much can be learned about an economy by studying the patterns of product use. Capital formation is involved in an ongoing adjustment to demand. As will be demonstrated in a later analysis, the distribution of demand relies on total personal income per group and total personal consumption.

International migration is a phenomenon that can impact an economy significantly. The lack of immigration into the United States (U.S.) during World War I and World War II is contrasted by Kuznets (1966) with migration in the periods of 1901–1910 and 1911–1920. More detailed research reveals that the period 1900–1914 represents a period of population increase through immigration into the U.S.

Kuznets (1966) describes a process of transition by which the economies of nations become developed. The convergence of previously mentioned factors and human capital, capital, and entrepreneurship sets the stage for a transition to development.

An adequate theory of economic growth is unlikely given the differences in populations and insufficient data. Large differences in per capita income indicate a variety of differences in capital resources (Kuznets 1965b). Developed economies are living, dynamic entities with changing structures. Kuznets (1965b) proposed that shifts in industrial structures and the labor force distribution be the primary focus of economic analysis. He proposed that only secondary attention be given to the industrial distribution of income. In this analysis of the U.S. economy, characteristics that provide mutually exclusive categories for analysis are used (the author).

A developing economy shows a capacity to provide a growing population with the commodities and services necessary to accommodate the population's needs (Kuznets 1973). Kuznets summarizes his estimates of developed countries' consumer consumption expenditures, and consumption of services (71 percent), capital formation (21 percent), and government consumption (8 percent). This breakdown off the components of aggregate demand will be tested in Part I, Analysis of Aggregate Demand.

Kuznets (1973) drew attention to shifting age structures that have long term consequences for economic growth. This will be demonstrated in Part II, Data and Calculations.

The relationship between capital and consumption is important. Capital stock contributes to output and productivity. For an increase in capital to be effective, it must be accompanied by consumption at the elevated levels of output. Without increased demand for output, capital formation slows. Kuznets (1973) advanced the view that the slower growth of total product in the pre-World War II era was associated with slower population growth rate.

Kuznets (1973) maintains that "technology requires greater education, different patterns of organization of land and agriculture, and a variety of changes in both agricultural and non-agricultural institutions (p. 79–80)." "Social feasibility," another requirement for change, has been difficult to assess in both general and empirically testable forms (p. 91).

Kuznets (1973) concluded that there are six basic characteristics of modern economic growth: (1) high rates of growth in developed countries along with high rates of growth in population and per capita product, (2) growth in the rate of productivity, (3) structural transformation occurred at a high rate, (4) the structures of society and ideologies changed rapidly (examples are urbanization and secularization), (5) developed nations acquire the capacity (and use it) to become international in the scope of their economies, and (6) the partial effects of large modern economies fell short of the levels feasible with the potential of modern technology.

Modern economic growth (still expanding) is somewhat limited. The transition from an underdeveloped nation to a developed nation has been slowed and may be further slowed by the process of transition. This led to a widening gap between developed nations and underdeveloped countries (Kuznets 1966). The presence of natural resources currently leads to the development of some nations.

Kuznets (1979) maintained that there has been a mutual relationship between economic growth and innovation. Growth in per capita income has been supported by measures of nutrition, health, longevity, increased choice of consumer goods, and development of energy supplies. Such changes have occurred through the application of new knowledge, innovation, and social evolution.

As one moves from less developed nations to more developed nations, the agriculture sector has decreased in size, and the manufacturing and service sectors have increased in size (Kuznets 1959). The phenomenon of urbanization has been accompanied by a shift from agriculture to manufacturing (1965b). Developed nations feature innovation and possible growth (Kuznets 1979).

This chapter emphasizes that economic growth (especially in the area of personal consumption) depends on the number of individuals receiving income, their mean annual income, and their ethnicity, sex, and age group. The individual who receives income is obligated to pay taxes, to follow the "consumption imperative," and engage in human and organizational efforts to increase the value of his/her labor (Schulz 1960 and Becker 1965) that maintain a vibrant economy.

In light of the concerns of previous authors, this chapter addresses three considerations. The first is the concern of having sufficient data of a usable nature. Second, inside the nation-state the author proposes a revised basis for calculating income. The basis that will be used is the individual receiving income. This unit of analysis is judged to be superior to estimates of per capita income because per capita income spreads income over the entire population of a nation-state. Finally, further disaggregates the population receiving income into the proportion of the group that has income, and the annual mean income for sex, age, and ethnic groups, resulting in mutually distinct groups with mutually exclusive mean incomes.

Robert Solow, in his Nobel Lecture (1987) and Radcliffe Lectures (1969) (1988) proposed a single-sector growth model. Of note to his writing is that it did not rely on empirical characterization of mean personal income and the number earning income. This does not preclude that capital and output are components of growth that respond to increases in demand. Measurements of changes in output are coincident or closely associated in time with personal income ($r = .96$, $N = 11$, $p = 0.00$) and personal consumption ($r = .95$, $N = 11$, $p = 0.00$) despite a small N. Similarly, both personal income ($r = .99$, p = 0.00) and personal consumption (r = .99, p = 0.00) are highly correlated with nonfarm productivity (N = 34).

Julian Simon (1989) noted that correlations between the rate of population growth and the rate of growth of per capita income were rarely significant. The lack of correlation between two variables has usually been a strong indication that the variables do not influence each other. Barlow (1994) attempts to add lagged fertility to the current rate of population growth for use in predicting current per capita income growth. Barlow does this to make explicit both the short-term and long-term effects of population growth. The correlation between population growth and per capita gross domestic product (for 144 observations over the same six year period) yields a result of no correlation. Barlow (1994) did find a significant relationship between lagged fertility (in a six year average) beginning 17 years before the start of the period over which economic growth is measured.

Perhaps the most relevant perspective to the estimations developed herein is that of Behrman (2001):

> For both good conditional predictions and good policy formation regarding most dimensions of population change and economic development, a perspective firmly grounded in understanding the micro determinants . . . is essential (p. 371).

Disaggregating the basis for personal income allows the estimation of total personal income, total disposable personal income, and total personal consumption.

TESTING AGGREGATE DEMAND

This chapter will use estimates of personal income to develop empirical estimates of actual personal income, actual personal consumption and actual aggregate demand. The relationships of the terms in the aggregate demand equation are tested in the text (Box 3.2) and tables (Table 3.1). The aggregate demand equation is in Box 3.1:

Aggregate Demand		Personal Consumption		Government Capital Expenditures		Gross Domestic Private Investment		Net Exports	
AD_{xt}	=	PC_{xt}	+	GOV_{xt}	+	$GDPI_{xt}$	+	Z_{xt}	(3.1)

The correlations between AD, PC, GOV, and GDPI are all r = .96 or above. This indicates a great deal of parallelism between the values for these variables. Net exports (Z) is the only variable negatively related to AD, PC, GOV, and GDPI indicating an inverse relationship with those variables.

This relationship is a mathematical equality with four independent variables and their coefficients added to the term for aggregate demand. Thus, the adjusted $R^2 = 1.00$. The values for Beta in the standardized equation are presented in Table 3.1. The *beta coefficients* are the regression coefficients obtained by first standardizing all of the variables to a mean of zero (0) and a standardized coefficient of one (1). These coefficients allow the relative contribution of each independent (predictor) variable to the variation in the dependent variable to be assessed. For example, a variation of one in the value of the standardized variable PC means that there will be a variation of 0.692 in the dependent variable AD.

The contribution of each of the independent variables to aggregate demand is: the variation of PC by one standard deviation results in a change in AD by 0.692 standard deviations. The variation in government investment expenditures (GOV) by one standard deviation results in a variation in AD by 0.186 standard deviations. Variation of GDPI by one standard deviation results in variation of AD by 0.163 standard deviation. Variation in the standard deviation of Z by one standard deviation results in a variation in AD by 0.041 standard deviation. These variations may be expressed in terms of percents.

TABLE 3.1: Correlation Matrix (N=77)

	AD	PC	GOV	GDPI
PC	.999*	—		
GOV	.997*	.996*	—	
GDPI	.976*	.966*	.964*	—
Z	-.859*	-.873*	-.857*	-.837*

*p = 0.00

TABLE 3.2: Beta Weights

Variables	Beta
PC	.692
GOV	.186
GDPI	.163
Z	.041

TABLE 3.3: Means and Standard Deviations (N=77)

Variables	Standard Deviation	Mean
AD	3442.7	2766.3
PC	2382.1	1824.8
GOV	641.9	530.6
GDPI	559.5	472.7
Z	-61.9	142.0

What insights do this equation and its beta weights present? First, and most prominent, is the fact that AD is dependent on PC for slightly over 69% of its variation. The knowledge that personal consumption is so much of a part of economic activity will help us to understand the sources of that activity. The variables with smaller betas each contribute smaller percentages to the variation in AD. For detailed variables, means and standard deviations see Table 3.2.

The aggregate demand equation and the beta coefficients emphasize the role of personal consumption in the U.S. economy. To disaggregate the term disposable personal income equations in Box 3.2 with defined values in Box 3.3 are suggested:

$$\sum_{x=1}^{x=n} ((\overline{PI}_{XT} - (\overline{tx}_{xt} \pm \overline{s}_{xt} \pm \overline{db}_{xt})) = \sum_{x=1}^{x=n} DPI_{XT} \qquad (3.2)$$

Definitions of Terms In Box 3.2

$\overline{PI}_{XT}$ = mean personal income of group x at time t (3.3)

$\overline{tx}_{xt}$ = mean taxes of group x at time t

$\overline{s}_{xt}$ = mean savings of group x at time t (net deposits or withdrawals)

$\overline{db}_{xt}$ = debt of group x at time t (net debt acquisition or payments)

DPI_{XT} = disposable income of group x at time t

group x = 0, 1,2,…n

DATA AND CALCULATIONS

To calculate the estimations income data were used from the Current Population Survey (CPS), Annual Social and Economic Supplement (ASEC) (1967–2000). The ASEC contains the information on labor force and demographics found in the CPS and additional information on income, migration, noncash benefits and work experience. The research focused on four variables from the March Supplement. Those were: mean income by sex, age, and ethnicity, and the number of individuals receiving income for each group. Additional data were used from the Bureau of the Census, and the CPS, on the number of individuals in each sex, age, and ethnic group in the United States (U.S.). Table 1 presents the data on population, number receiving personal income, mean constant dollar income, ethnicity, age grouping and sex.

An example of data used is in Table 3.4:

TABLE 3.4: Population, Number of Individuals with Personal Income, and Mean Constant Dollar Personal Income for 2000 by Ethnicity, Age, and Sex

Ethnicity & Age Group	Population	Number with Personal Income	Mean Personal Income	Ethnicity & Age Group	Population	Number with Personal Income	Mean Personal Income
White Non-Hispanic Males				Hispanic Males			
15–24	13,002,127	10,226,000	$13,666	15–24	2,933,485	2,016,000	$13,800
25–34	12,518,851	11,979,000	41,539	25–34	2,722,095	2,711,000	27,056
35–44	16,226,416	15,737,000	54,461	35–44	2,519,989	2,481,000	31,982
45–54	14,112,168	14,080,000	59,919	45–54	1,517,684	1,472,000	33,012
55–64	9,200,538	8,707,000	54,901	55–64	813,997	833,000	28,046
65 & over	12,134,022	11,672,000	31,211	65 & over	816,647	737,000	17,223

Ethnicity & Age Group	Population	Number with Personal Income	Mean Personal Income	Ethnicity & Age Group	Population	Number with Personal Income	Mean Personal Income
White Non-Hispanic Females				Hispanic Females			
15–24	12,329,839	9,727,000	$11,244	15–24	2,841,240	1,702,000	$10,111
25–34	12,553,785	11,399,000	25,867	25–34	2,594,060	2,201,000	19,026
35–44	16,190,407	15,055,000	29,343	35–44	2,422,200	2,051,000	19,381
45–54	14,383,623	13,796,000	30,215	45–54	1,586,206	1,393,000	21,512
55–64	9,804,961	9,068,000	23,658	55–64	945,903	744,000	17,281
65 & over	16,963,405	15,256,000	16,414	65 & over	1,120,943	989,000	10,047
African-American Males				Other Males			
15–24	2,777,693	1,649,000	$10,817	15–24	946,781	677,000	$12,20
25–24	2,343,633	2,086,000	33,145	25–24	973,348	1,151,000*	39,539
35–44	2,533,454	2,501,000	33,043	35–44	1,009,266	1,096,000*	56,782
45–54	1,790,106	1,834,000	33,483	45–54	754,139	821,000*	53,264
55–64	999,232	977,000	35,595	55–64	429,385	421,000	45,336
65 & over	1,111,755	1,076,000	20,090	65 & over	410,441	474,000*	22,370
African-American Females				Other Females			
15–24	2,758,273	2,012,000	$10,282	15–24	950,396	663,000	$11,658
25–24	2,613,931	2,643,000	22,705	25–24	1,120,773	1,034,000	26,507
35–44	2,882,745	2,890,000	25,062	35–44	1,109,290	1,081,000	26,469
45–54	2,160,723	2,162,000	28,135	45–54	861,553	840,000	26,249
55–64	1,315,793	1,207,000	20,388	55–64	491,287	416,000	23,553
65 & over	1,715,030	1,612,000	12,341	65 & over	563,050	511,000	13,274

* Numbers with personal income > than the subgroup population are excessive. They are derived values and should not exceed .99 as large.

$$(NPY_x)(\overline{Y}_x) = GRPY_x \qquad (3.4)$$

$\overline{Y}_x$ = mean personal income for group x

NPY_x = number with personal income for a group x

$GRPY_x$ = total group personal income for all groups x

x = group identified by sex, age, and ethnicity. x = 1, 2…n

Once $GRPY_x$ has been calculated for each x, the results can be summed to estimated total personal income (ESTPINC).

$$ESTPINC = \sum_{x=1}^{x=n} GRPY_x$$

Annual calculations were made for variables 1967–2000 in Box 3.3 from 1967–2000 and 1967–2011 using Current Population Survey ASEC calculations.

Table 3.4 shows that income varies by age group, sex, and ethnicity. The number of individuals with personal income (NPY) is multiplied by the average personal income for each population group in each sex, age, and ethnic category to obtain the group's total personal income. When this calculation is completed for all sex, age, and ethnic groups the data can be summed to obtain total personal income (see Box 3.4).

The equation is designed to demonstrate the components of total personal income and variables that account for some of the variation in personal income and personal consumption. Three lines of proof will be presented.

First, Table 3.3 provides descriptive evidence on how the size of population groups varies by ethnicity, sex, age, and mean income. This evidence is taken from the 2000 Current Population Survey, Annual Social and Economic Supplement (ASEC). Table 3.3 illustrates part of this variation across ethnic, sex and age groups, and across annual mean incomes. These variations affect the total income of these groups and generate changes in total personal income, total personal consumption, and total aggregate demand.

Figure 3.1 presents information on the numbers of males in specific age groups during 1976–2015. The data is presented to demonstrate the level of variation that occurs within the population regarding the size of the age groups in a single ethnicity and gender group. The aggregate population consists of a diversity of ethnic, age, and sex groups. When the dimensions of and variations in mean income, population, and population receiving income are also included in the analysis, the basic variables that can be used to estimate the components of total income are all accounted for.

Figure 3.1 demonstrates the variations that may occur in the number of individuals in specific sex, age, and ethnic groups over time. Such variations are components of the variation in group income.

The populations for the sub-groups aged 15–24, 25–34, and 35–44 of white, Non-Hispanic males reached their low points in 1996, 2006, and 2016 respectively. They reached their peak points in 1979, 1987, and 1998, respectively. Estimated losses in group population size and estimated gains of the occurred in the amounts in Table 3.5:

The numbers of persons receiving personal income and their mean personal incomes varies by sex, age, and ethnicity in the data from the website of the Current Population Survey, Annual Social and Economic Supplement. Demographers' and economists' perceptions of income growth and population growth have been limited by the variables of per capita income and the fertility rate. Per capita income spreads the income received by only certain individuals over the total population of a jurisdiction. It is important to note that the selected categories in Table 3.1 allow clear distinctions between different groups of the income-receiving population. However, other categorizations are also possible. Specifically, education level could be used as another characteristic upon which categories could be based on nation-state. As such, the use of per capita income understates the income of income-receiving members of the population.

TABLE 3.5: Population Gains and Losses of Selected Male Groups in Millions of Persons*

Age Group	Year of Peak Population	Year of Low Population	Gain or Loss of Population in (millions of persons)
15–24	1979	1996	-5.876
25–34	1987	2006	-4.352
35–44	1998	2016	-4.209
45–54	2008	2020	-3.370
55–64	Increasing from 1992 to 2018		+6.734
65 & over	Increasing from 1976 to 2025		+10.912

*Calculations based on live births, and survival rates, National Center for Health Statistics and Social Security data respectively

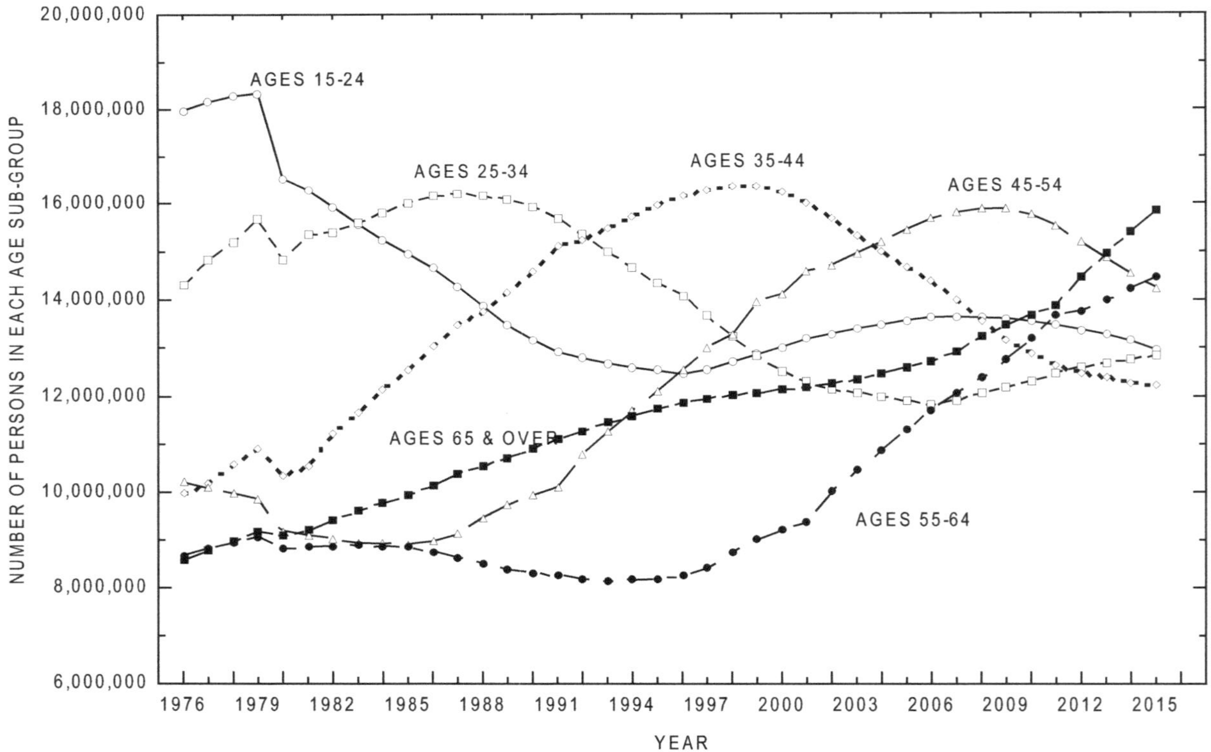

Sources:Current Population Survey, Annual Social and Economic Supplement (ASEC), Bureau of the Census

FIGURE 3.1: Number of White, Non-Hispanic Males by Age Subgroups: 1976-2015

Secondly, the fertility rate spreads all live births over a given age range of females. Young females are giving birth with increasing frequency. To accurately count births, the recommended statistic is live births by mother's age and child's sex. The combined use of annual live births, sex of the new-born, and the interpolated decennial survival rates provides accurate population numbers until the survival rates decompose. In the U.S. a survival rate is prepared for the year at the beginning of each decade. Annual survival rates can be interpolated from decennial values.

THE RELATIONSHIP BETWEEN PERSONAL INCOME AND ESTIMATED PERSONAL INCOME

The next step of the validation consists of correlating the actual total personal income with the estimated personal income values. This results in the correlation coefficient between the two variables being r = .99 (p = 0.00, N = 34). This is sufficient to validate the similarity of actual personal income and ESTPINC.

Figure 3.2: Correlation of Actual Personal Income and Estimated Personal Income

Figure 3.2 shows a near-perfect relationship between actual personal income and the estimated personal income featured earlier in this chapter. Estimates of personal income by this method accurately predicted the occurrence of recessions in 1975–76, 1980–81, and 1990–92.

SUMMARY AND CONCLUSIONS

This chapter demonstrates how estimates for personal income using data (on ethnicity, sex, age, ethnicity of the income-receiving population, and annual mean group income) from the Current Population Survey (CPS), Annual Social and Economic Supplement (ASEC). That a personal income estimate can be prepared demonstrates that variables indicating the numbers of individuals receiving income, disaggregated by their sex, age, ethnicity, and mean income affect actual and estimated mean personal income. The variation in these components accurately pinpoints the years in which economic upturns and downturns occur.

The mechanism that occurs when group population growth and income growth are present is a decrease in inventories (if inventories are available). If demand increases and remains at an increased or increasing level, production increases to meet the new demand and inventories are adjusted to acceptable

ACTUAL PERSONAL INCOME = -4585. + 2.0551 * ESTPINC

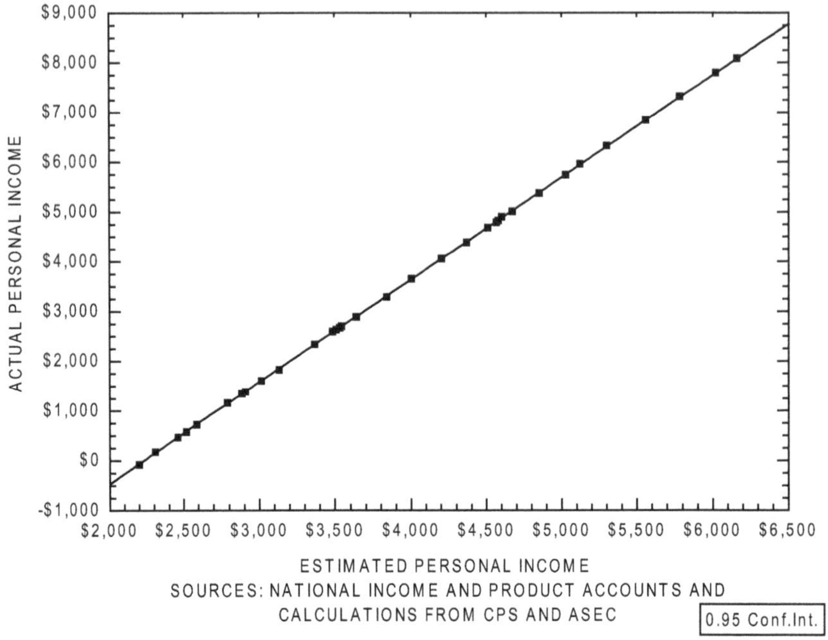

FIGURE 3.2: Actual Personal Income vs. Estimated Personal Income

levels. Additional productivity may absorb the increase in demand. If increased productivity is not present or is inadequate to accommodate increased demand, additional gross domestic private investment may be required. Dollars for gross domestic private investment are obtained from capital. Capital is derived from investment and savings. At the time of the increase in total income, there is potential for declining inventories, increased gross domestic private investment, and/or increased imports. Currently there is not enough demand so that some form of demand may have to be introduced by the government.

If group population level(s) and total income level(s) decline, inventories may expand or decline and there will likely be a reduction in gross domestic private investment. Total income levels affect gross domestic private investment through disposable personal income and personal consumption.

Growth in disposable personal income and personal consumption means that business income will increase. Homeostasis is reached in the unlikely situation that all forms of consumption and the product supply are in homeostatic balance. Aggregate disposable personal income and personal

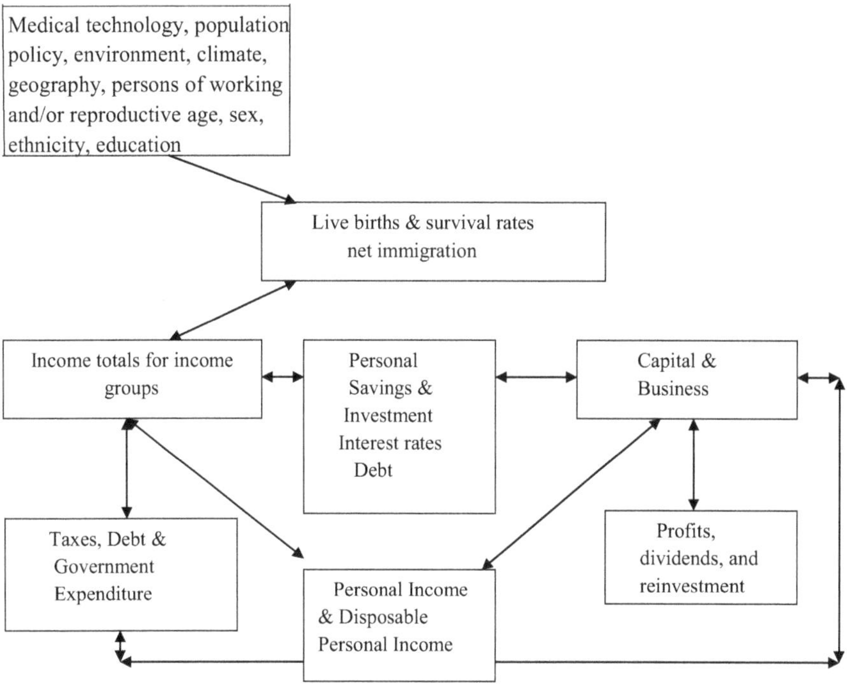

FIGURE 3.3: A Simplified Model of United States Demography and Economic Change*

consumption are rooted in mutually exclusive income-earning groups defined by age, sex, ethnicity, mean group income, and numbers of individuals receiving income. Figure 3.3 provides a schematic systems model that has blends the results from this research with the figure presented by Bloom and Canning (2001, Figure 8.6, pp. 185).

It should be noted that several quantities in this diagram might vary in both a positive or negative direction given a reference value (i.e. live births, immigration and emigration, average incomes used to calculate total income, personal consumption, capital and business, reinvestment, savings and investment, interest rates, net government expenditures, debt, and year-to-year taxes).

This systems model is made possible by pursuing the disaggregation suggested by Bloom and Canning (2001), but in a different manner based on available data.

CHAPTER 4

The Events Leading to and Following the Great Recession

Both the Great Depression and the Great Recession started with a housing boom and a housing bust followed by a peak in foreclosures. The combination of investment institutions and banks was made possible by the final rescinding of the Glass-Steagall Act in 1999. This act separated investment and commercial banking activities. At the time of the Depression, "improper banking activity," or what was considered to be overzealous commercial bank involvement in stock market investment, was deemed the main culprit in the financial crash. The housing boom that ended in 1929 has not been given a sufficient amount of attention. This was a direct result of an increase in the number of immigrants between 1905 and 1914. The average age of immigrants at that time was thirty through thirty-three years of age. Lagging immigration 16 years yields a correlation between immigration and housing starts of $r = .63$, $p = 0.002$, $N=22$ (see Figure 4.1).

Figure 4.1 confirms the variation in immigrants during the greatest periods of housing increases) and declines from (1921–1925) and (1926–1933) respectively.

DATA AND EVENTS FROM THE RECENT PAST

The data on foreclosures were calculated from data purchased from the Mortgage Bankers Association. The data used here reflect non-seasonally adjusted foreclosures; these data were quarterly in their original form but were converted to an annual format. The housing starts data were obtained from the United States Census Bureau and were also converted from a quarterly to an annual format.

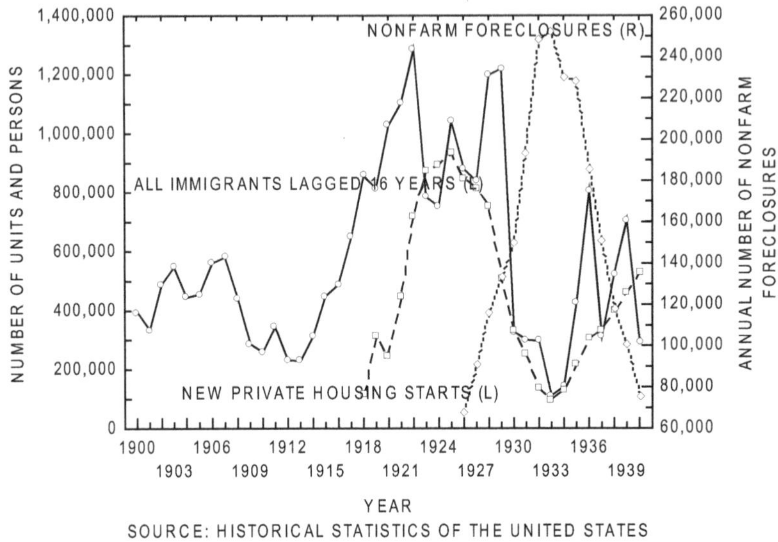

FIGURE 4.1: Immigrants Lagged 16 Years, Private Housing Starts, and Non-farm Foreclosures

Figure 4.2 presents annual data from 2000 through 2010. Figure 4.2 is deceiving as the Y-axes have different scales. The left Y-axis for annual housing starts peaks in 2005 at 2,148,000 and then declines to 559,000 in 2010. This rapid decline in housing starts weakened the retail market for all materials used to make houses and for the contents of homes (dishwashers, refrigerators, furnishings, etc.). The low effective demand for housing had a ripple effect throughout the U.S. economy.

According to demographic information, additional phenomena will emerge in the coming years. People past the age of 65 become more likely to die. From 2010–2040, approximately 104.174 million individuals will transition into this category or pass away. As these individuals die they will leave behind a large volume of existing stock for resale. This high level of used housing stock will make it unnecessary to build new housing stock at the pre-2000 rates and levels. As a result, the proportion of used housing stock on the housing and rental market will increase. Multiple housing units (3–5+ units) are expected to assume a greater proportion of the housing and rental market as these units will accommodate the needs of lower-income families. The decline of housing prices in particular regions of the country will affect the movement into used housing.

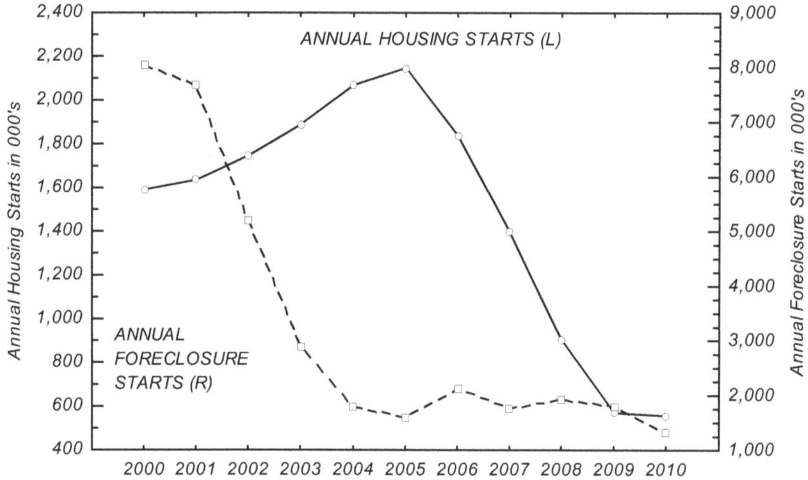

SOURCES: U.S. BUREAU OF THE CENSUS, HOUSING STARTS 1-5+ UNITS; ANNUAL FORECLOSURE STARTS CALCULATED FROM MATERIAL PROVIDED BY THE MORTGAGE BANKERS ASSOCIATION

FIGURE 4.2: Annual Housing Starts in the U.S. Compared to Annual Foreclosure Starts in the U.S., 2000-2010

The number of annual foreclosure starts declined from 8.036 million in 2000 to 1.333 million in 2010. Annual housing starts increased from a low of 1.568 million in 2000 to a peak of 2.068 million in 2005. The housing bust then began in 2005, and that figure declined to 0.554 million starts in 2009.

A DETAILED LOOK

The Financial Crisis Inquiry Report (FCIR, 2011) developed by the Financial Crisis Inquiry Commission (FCIC) contains two sections. One features the views of the majority of the Commission and the other features the dissenting views of the Commission minority. The author suggests that the dissenting view addresses the roots of the crisis and the majority view describes how the crisis manifested itself. The National Mortgage Association (Fannie Mae) was originated in 1938 by the Reconstruction Finance Corporation to purchase mortgages insured by the Federal Housing Authority (FHA). Eventually, loans from the Veterans Housing Administration (VHA) were added to its portfolio.

Congress passed important housing legislation that was signed into law in 1992. This legislation is referred to as Title XIII of the Housing and Community Development Act of 1992 (GSE Act). The purpose of the act was to give low- and moderate-income borrowers better access to mortgages through Fannie Mae and Federal Home Loan Mortgage Corporation (Freddie Mac) (CICR, 2011, p. 452). The GSE Act deviated from its original intent of managing of a secondary market of prime mortgages. Fannie Mae was formed during the New Deal to buy mortgages from banks and loan originators. As a result, the banks and loan originators had access to additional funds with which they could grant additional mortgage loans. In 1968, Fannie Mae was authorized to sell its shares and become a government-sponsored-enterprise (GSE), enabling it to maintain a liquid secondary market in mortgages. In 1970, Freddie Mac also became another GSE. Both Freddie Mac and Fannie Mae applied conservative lending standards to mortgages they purchased. These standards included down payments of 10 to 20 percent and credit standards for borrowers. However, this began to change in the early 1990's.

The GSE Act (1992) mandated a new mission for Fannie Mae, Freddie Mac, and the Department of Housing and Urban Development (HUD). Fannie and Freddie were to provide a secondary market for affordable housing (AH) mortgages. HUD was assigned the role of setting annual goals for low and middle income (LMI) mortgage generation. HUD established percentage levels of all mortgages that were required to be LMI mortgages. Twenty-seven percent of loans made by GSEs had to be at or below 80 percent of area median income (AMI). The following table (Table 4.1) presents how those goals changed over the years (CFCR, pp. 454). The goals were met by Fannie and Freddie for almost every year after 1996.

Most subprime and Alt-A mortgages in which Fannie and Freddie invested were high risk loans. Most subprime borrowers have blemished financial records, and tend to have a FICO (credit score) scores of less than 660. Prior to the early 1990s, the Federal Housing Authority (FHA) and specialized subprime lenders would not issue such loans. In contrast, an Alt-A loan may have an adjustable rate, offer zero interest, stipulate a term longer than a 30 year term, be used for rental housing, and have a high loan-to-value ratio (with a small or negligible down payment). The causes of the significant decline in lending standards 1992–2008 period are clear. More than 27 million subprime and Alt-A loans had been issued by 2009. Fannie and Freddie's portfolios included a total of 32 million loans. Immediately prior to the financial crisis 12 million subprime and Alt-A mortgage loans were active.

The role of HUD in setting AH goals and in determining the ways in which these goals will be used to guide the mortgage lending by banks in the 1992–2008 period was central to the development of the bubble and burst that initiated and prolonged the housing crisis (Table 4.1).

TABLE 4.1: HUD Goals for LMI Mortgages, 1992–2008

Year	Percent of Mortgage Purchases to be AH
1992–3	30 %
1995	42
2000	50
2008	56

Source: CFCR

The housing crisis has manifested itself in many ways. From 1995 to 2005 housing prices rose by more than 67 percent (National Association of Realtors, 2010). The average price of existing homes rose from $135,800 in the second-quarter of 1995 to a peak average national price of $227,100 in the second-quarter of 2005. One factor that contributed to the financial crisis was the intentional inflation of prices. A realtor selling a used or new home for an owner or builder would have the home assessed. Assessors were pressured, to increase their assessments; as a result, sales prices increased to along with the loans provided by banks. This procedure worked very well for individuals interested in 'flipping' houses, a process whereby the margin between the purchase and sales prices of houses are leveraged to generate profits in a short period of time.

The housing crisis became systematic. The Mortgage Bankers Association (MBA), a group of independent mortgage bankers, agreed to participate in a HUD program called the "Best Practices Initiative." At that time the Community Reinvestment Act (CRA) applied only to government-insured banks. The CRA did not apply to the MBA. In September 1994 the MBA signed a three-year agreement. The agreement permitted individual banks to develop their own agreements with HUD and stated that the MBA would work on fair-lending issues with HUD. By 1998, there were 117 Best Practice signatories.

The most important participant in the "Best Practices Initiative" was the Countrywide Funding Corporation. This firm made a number of multi-billion dollar commitments followed by a trillion dollar commitment (789 billion of which was met) to provide loans to low-income and minority families.

The number of non-traditional mortgages (NTMs) increased substantially between 1993 and 2008. The CRA, adopted in 1977, facilitated that expansion. When the CRA was revised in 1995, CRA insured banks were obligated to purchase or make "flexible and innovative" loans in their assessment areas. Fannie Mae, Freddie Mac, and CRA entered the same AH territory. Under the CRA, community organizations and lenders entered into over 446 agreements totaling over 4.5 trillion dollars in local investments (CFCR, 2011, pp. 526).

The actors involved in creating the financial crisis included home loan seekers, lending institutions, assessors, investment houses, rating agencies, firms securitizing mortgages, mortgage insurers, HUD, Fannie Mae, Freddie Mac, the FHA, CRA, and investors. Their motives extended from increasing the number of AH units to earning profits.

The demand for securitized mortgages grew along with mortgage indebtedness in the U.S. Mortgage debt increased from 5.3 trillion dollars in 2001 to 10.5 trillion dollars in 2007 (CFCR, 2011, pp. 74). Household debt averaged 91,500 dollars in 2001 and grew to an average of 149,000 dollars in 2007. With the advent and growth of securitization, mortgages were packaged, repackaged, insured, and divided, until the owner of the mortgage was no longer identifiable. These products were finally sold to eager buyers.

Many home loans entered the securitization process soon after borrowers signed the papers. In many cases, houses entered the market with inordinately high prices. Realtors and assessors colluded to inflate housing prices in a rising market. As a result, many new homeowners found themselves in a falling housing market in which their houses were worth much less than they had paid for them. As housing prices rose between 2001 and 2007, enterprising individuals took advantage of rising prices and "flipped" houses. These individuals bought desirable houses off the market only to sell them at a higher price. Some of these individuals were affected when the housing bubble burst.

Traditional mortgages (TMs), those with 30-year terms and down payments of 20 percent, were gradually replaced by NTMs. With few government restrictions, lending standards declined and the number of NTMs increased. Interest only mortgages accounted for approximately one-quarter of all mortgages in the first six months of 2005. A shadow banking industry developed. "Option ARM" mortgages were developed which had low- or no-documentation requirements.

The Federal Reserve failed "to ensure the safety and soundness of the nation's banking and financial system and to protect the credit rights of consumers" (CFCR, 2011). Repeated warnings came from multiple sources. State regulators were blocked from halting abuses by the turf wars between the Office of Thrift Supervision and the Office of the Currency.

While U.S. banks recorded mortgages in their books, money came from international investors wishing to invest in mortgage-related securities. The passage of legislation in 2000 that banned the regulation of over-the-counter (OTC) derivatives by the federal and state government set the stage for the pipeline development. This lack of oversight was accompanied by negligence on the part of the market rating agencies on which investors relied. Moody's, for example, rated 45,000 mortgage-related securities as triple-A. In 2006, Moody's approved 30 triple-A securities per day. As a result, during and after the crash, 83 percent of triple-A rated mortgage securities were downgraded (CFCR, 2011, pp. *xxiv*).

A shadow banking industry developed. "Option ARM" mortgages with limited or no-documentation requirements were developed. Money market funds originated by Merrill Lynch, Fidelity, Vanguard, and other financial institutions were not protected by the Federal Deposit Insurance Corporation (FDIC). The amount of assets in such funds increased from 3 billion dollars in 1977, to 740 billion in 1995, to 1.8 trillion dollars in 2000. A second burgeoning shadow banking market was the market for repurchase agreements (repos). The repo market consisted of securities dealers who were selling treasury bonds with low returns to banks or other conservative investors while they invested in securities with higher interest rates. The securities dealers repurchased the treasuries within a short period (often one day) at a slightly higher price. The new parallel banking system provided cheaper financing and more money market funds, thereby increasing returns for investors and consumers. Banks and thrifts were threatened by these new sources of funds. As previously mentioned, money market mutual funds were not covered by deposit insurance.

Deregulation was a common practice of the federal government in the quarter-century prior to the housing crisis. The Depository Institutions Deregulatory and Monetary Control Act repealed the limits on interest rates charged by institutions. This act did not sufficiently reduce the competition between banks and thrifts; the gap between 1-year Treasury notes decreased from 5.5 percent in 1979 to 2.6 percent in 1994 (CFCR 2011, pp. 34). With the Garn-St. Germain Act, in 1982, interest rate issues were resolved by giving banks and thrifts the power to issue balloon-payment mortgages and adjustable rate mortgages (ARMs). In the short-term, the Act made a positive difference for consumers. However, in the long-term interest rates increased. Essentially, rising interest rates became the concern of consumers.

Banks pressured the Federal Reserve to adjust its rules (1987). Subsidiaries of bank holding companies could sell or hold securities that national banks were not allowed to underwrite or invest in. The Federal Reserve limited eligible security activities to 5 percent of assets or revenue. These restrictions were eventually relaxed. As early as 1997, bank-ineligible securities accounted for up to 25 percent of the assets or securities of a bank holding subsidiary. Banks were only permitted to loan 10 percent to one subsidiary and 20 percent to all subsidiaries. They could lend collateral and set terms on the basis of what market offerings (CFCR, 2011, pp. 35, pp.558). The Federal Reserve

TABLE 4.2: Year and Activities Added to National Banks Year Activities

1983	Securities
1988	Interest and Currency Exchange
1988	Stock Indices
1991	Precious metals
1994	Equity stocks

Source: CFCR

weakened or abolished other distinctions between traditional banking and the new securities of bank holding companies.

The regulator of nationally chartered banks, the Office of the Comptroller of the Currency (OCC), expanded the activities of national banks. These activities included underwriting, in addition to trading derivatives in accordance with the prices of defined assets. Table 4.2 lists the activities added to the portfolios' of national banks and the corresponding years in which the changes took effect.

Federal Reserve Chairman Alan Greenspan; and some regulators and some legislators favored the movement towards deregulation. In their opinion, deregulation would allow banking organizations to compete more effectively while offering better services to the public. That view was misguided and its prevalence contributed to the severity of the financial crisis.

Laws promulgated in 1968 and 1970 gave Fannie, Freddie, and Ginnie Mae options other than holding purchased mortgages. Ginnie Mae became the first organization to securitize mortgages while charging a fee to guarantee the timely payment of principal and interest. Freddie Mac bought mortgages starting in 1971. It pooled them and sold them as mortgage-backed-securities. Freddie Mac collected similar fees from lenders guaranteeing principal and interest. Fannie Mae followed after losing large amounts of money from a spike in interest rates. The importance of GSEs increased in the 1980s and 1990s, the market value of the FHA and the VHA declined, and the number of conventional mortgages increased (CFCR 2011, pp.39).

In purchasing loans from banks, mortgage companies, and the thrifts Fannie Mae (Fannie) and Freddie Mac (Freddie) either securitized and guaranteed loans or put them in their portfolios. Both organizations had special privileges including exemption from state and local taxes and a 2.5 billion dollar line of credit from the Department of the Treasury. In accordance with a special arrangement with the Federal Reserve (the Fed) they could borrow at rates that were almost as low as those paid by the Treasury. Banks, however, were strictly limited in the amount they could loan to a single borrower. They were also restricted in their investments in the debt obligations of other firms. GSEs held little capital that could protect against losses. They held 0.45 percent to guarantee of mortgage-backed securities and 2.5 percent to cover the mortgages in their portfolios. Four percent or more is typical for mortgages under conventional standards.

The political clout of Fannie and Freddie increased from 1999 to 2009. The two firms reported spending a total of 164 million dollars on lobbying. Political action committees and employees contributed 15 million dollars to campaigns during that period. Such tactics allowed them to avoid regulation (CFCR, 2011, pp.42–43). Fannie and Freddie had a near monopoly on the securitizing of fixed rate securities within permitted loan limits. Markets began to securitize adjustable-rate mortgages that GSEs were not permitted to buy. Investment banks and securities affiliates bundled loans from banks or other lenders and sold them to investors. Payments from the purchased securities acted as returns for investors. The securitized items included equipment leases, credit card debt, and money market funds (CFCR, 2011, pp. 42). Banks frequently accepted money from depositors and loaned it out as mortgages. The banks held the mortgages and received payments until the mortgage obligations were completed. With securitization mortgages were sold to firms that bundled them and sold them to investors. The direct relationship between borrowers and banks was gone.

Private securitization and structured finance securities (SFS) posed two benefits for investors: pooling and tranching. Pooling loans reduced the damage incurred by investors if one of the mortgages in the pool defaulted. Tranches were structured to allow buyers to customize their payments. Investors wishing to avoid risk would be paid off first in the event of a default. These tranches had lower yields. Investors seeking higher yields invested in lower-level tranches. Those with senior tranches were paid before those holding junior tranches. If payments declined sufficiently, those holding the lowest level of tranches were the first not to be paid (CFCR, 2011, pp. 43).

Investment bankers, investors, and lenders benefited from the securitization process. Lenders earned fees for making and selling loans. Investment banks received fees for preparing and selling mortgage-backed securities. They sold the securities to investors at prices that were higher than those of regular mortgage loans. To determine price, investors calculated the probability of default. Investors had to apply the probability of default to the different tranches.

At this point, the credit agencies became important to the process. The securities industry realized that it needed the rating agencies to rate its products. Moody's, Standard & Poor's (S&P), and Fitch became essential actors. Quantitative analyses became essential to the rating process. Triple-A ratings became the rule rather than the exception. The triple-A ratings were based on faulty analysis, but investors relied on these ratings. When banks sold loans they were not interested in loan quality.

Derivatives also became central to the financial crisis. Derivatives are financial contracts based on the value of aggregates of some underlying asset, index, or rate. Unlike securities, they are not used for investments or capital formation. They may be based on commodities of all types. They are used for speculation and risk hedging. Frequently, derivatives are used for exchange-traded futures and options or as OTC swaps. OTC derivatives are traded by bank holding companies and investment banks. This aspect of the financial system is neither regulated nor centralized (CFCR, 2011, pp. 44). Nevertheless, derivatives are an important part of the U.S. and global financial system.

Greenspan stated that he thought that OTC markets did well without CFTC regulation and advocated for fewer OTC regulations for exchange-traded derivatives, especially those handled by professional traders. Greenspan made these announcements both before and after Congress passed regulatory reforms in October 1998. In December 2000, President Clinton signed the Commodities Futures Modernization Act of 2000 (CFMA). This act deregulated the OTC market derivatives market and eliminated oversight by the Commodities Trading Commission (CFTC) and the Securities and Exchange Commission (SEC). At the end of 2000, the OTC derivatives market accounted for a notational amount of 95.2 trillion dollars. When the market peaked in June 2008, it accounted for 672.6 trillion dollars.

In Basel, Switzerland in 1988, the world's central banks loosened the capital requirements for mortgages and mortgage-backed securities. In 1966, the Basel Committee on Banking Supervision passed an amendment to Basel I that allowed banks to hedge their credit and market risks using derivatives. Thus, banks were allowed to hold less capital against trading and related activities. This increase in leverage, which occasionally rendered collateral entirely unnecessary requiring no collateral at all, permitted traders to purchase derivatives with a fraction of an investor's initial outlay (CFCR, 2011, pp.49).

Credit default swaps (CDSs) transferred the risk of default from the purchaser to the seller of the original debt. Bond and loan obligations were converted into debt securities. The purchaser of the debt security made regular payments to the seller during the lifetime of the swap. The seller was obliged to insure the investor against default or partial default. CDSs were not supervised by state insurance offices and were treated as unregulated OTC derivatives.

From 1998 to 2007, the assets of the five largest banks increased from 2.2 trillion dollars to 6.8 trillion dollars. The five largest investment banks had assets that grew from 1 trillion dollars to 4 trillion dollars during the same period.

Fed Chairman Greenspan claimed that in 1997 "The self interest of market participants generates private market regulation (CFCR, 2011, pp. 53)." Events of the financial crisis were to prove him wrong. In November 1999, the Gramm-Leach-Bilely Act (GLBA) was promulgated. Companies could underwrite and offer banking, securities, and insurance products. Advocates of the legislation thought that the resulting holding companies would be more profitable, safer, more consumer-friendly, and better able to compete with foreign banks that were already offering consolidated services.

Although the collapse of Enron and Worldcom preceded the collapse of Lehman Brothers in 2008, these earlier events were indicative of the interconnectedness of Wall Street firms. Investigations and legal proceedings revealed that Citigroup, Merrill Lynch, JP Morgan, and assorted Wall Street banks had helped Enron to hide its debt before collapsing. Enron generated false earnings and falsified debt as sales and derivative transactions. Citigroup, Merrill Lynch, JP Morgan, Lehman Brothers, CIBC, and Bank of America were responsible for another 6.9 billion dollars in class-action lawsuits (CFCR, 2011).

Prior to the subprime crisis and the advent of computerized-credit scoring, relied on other criteria when underwriting mortgages. Other criteria were important to the underwriting of mortgages. These criteria included creditworthiness, income capacity, liquid capital necessary to cover down payment and other loan costs, and collateral, and the value of a property and its condition. Borrowers were evaluated individually by local offices.

Outstanding debts in U.S. credit markets rose by 300 percent in the 1980s. In 1990, debt reached 13.8 trillion dollars. GSE debt and securitized mortgages accounted for 11 percent of this figure. In the 1990s, banks, mortgage companies, and Wall Street firms began securitizing mortgages. More of the mortgages became subprime. Funding for mortgages changed in the forty-year period from 1970 to 2010. The proportion of mortgages issued by savings and loans institutions peaked at approximately 88 percent of all mortgages in 1973. Beginning in 1978, there was an extreme drop occurred, with savings and loans institutions issuing only 4 percent of all mortgages in 2010. Government-sponsored enterprises issued approximately 6 percent of all mortgages in 1970. This figure increased to approximately 54 percent of all mortgages in 2010. Compared with other types of organizations commercial banks and

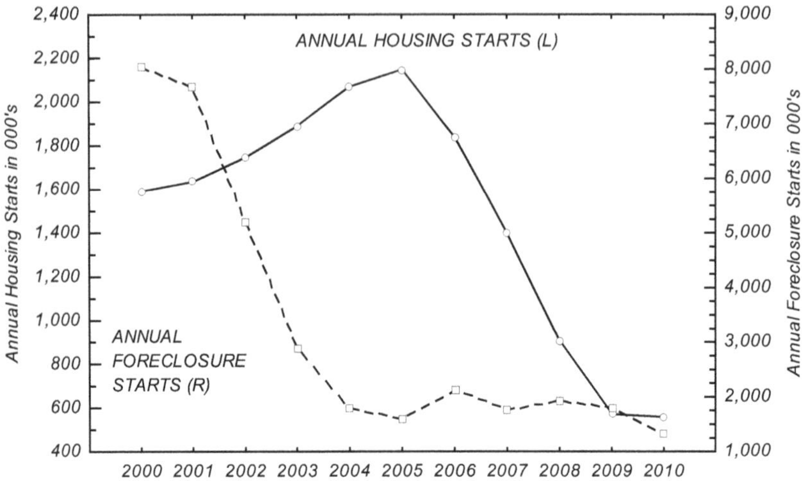

SOURCES: U.S. BUREAU OF THE CENSUS, HOUSING STARTS 1-5+ UNITS; ANNUAL FORECLOSURE STARTS CALCULATED FROM MATERIAL PROVIDED BY THE MORTGAGE BANKERS ASSOCIATION

FIGURE 4.3: Subprime Mortgage Originations, 1996-2008

other firms issued a more consistent proportion of mortgages. These institutions issued 39 percent of all mortgages in 1970. That percent declined to 29 percent in 2010. Non-agency sources issued approximately 1 percent of all mortgages in 1983 and 13 percent in 2010 (CFCR, 2011, pp. 69).

In 1989, the RTC was formed to reduce some of the residue from the savings and loan crisis. Of the 402 billion dollars at stake, the RTC was able to sell only 6.1 billion dollars to Fannie and Freddie. The problem was that most of the residue did not meet GSE standards. Some of these loans had documentation or servicing problems. Having decided they did not have the resources to sell off assets one by one, The RTC officials turned to the private sector and contracted with financial and real estate professionals to securitize approximately 25 billion dollars of residential assets.

In the early 2000s, the number of securitized mortgages, many of them were subprime, began to increase. Wall Street firms packaged loans that did not meet the standards of Fannie and Freddie. This packaging resulted in securities that were so complicated investors could not understand them. The response was a reliance on ratings agencies for securities ratings. During the periods directly before and during the crisis investors retained their faith in rating agencies. In the first decade after the millennium, securitizations became more complicated. Initially they were divided into two tranches, the greater risk was assumed by those investing in the more risky tranches. As private securitization evolved, securities were divided into more and more tranches that accommodated alternative levels of risk. This accommodated willing investors.

Federal agencies paid an increasing amount of attention to illegal lending practices. The regulatory system, however, was not able to protect borrowers at the national level. The Truth in Lending Act (1968) authorized the Federal Reserve to write rules regulating mortgages for all lenders. Unfortunately, the responsibility of enforcing the rules was divided among many financial regulators. The Federal Trade Commission (FTC) was designated to enforce regulations for non-bank lenders. While this looked good on paper, the FTC did not have the staff to police mortgage issues. Meanwhile, the Federal Reserve did not exert its authority in this and other areas until after the housing bubble burst.

The Homeownership and Equity Protection Act (HOEPA), passed in 1994, addressed abusive and predatory lending practices affecting low-income borrowers. Communities of low-income borrowers were being taken advantage of by home improvement contractors, second-mortgage lenders, and finance companies selling high-rate second mortgages. The interest rate eligibility standards were high enough to prevent most low-income individuals from qualifying for loans. Despite such practices, HOEPA appealed to the Fed to prohibit and punish wrongdoers.

The Fed did not act on its legislative prerogatives before the housing bust. While both the Fed and HUD backed legislative provisions related to balloon payments, advance collection of insurance payments, stronger enforcement of existing laws, and non-regulatory approaches such as consumer education and counseling, Congress failed to act on any of these recommendations.

Sheila Bair was the assistant secretary for financial institutions at the FDIC. She noticed that poor-quality loans reduced the market shares of traditional banks. This pressure on banks and thrifts encouraged them to follow in the footsteps of lending institutions that were creating poor-quality loans. Relevant legislation was introduced in Congress but it received resistance from the mortgage industry and some members of Congress. Blair became interested in convincing the industry to accept a recommended set of best practices. These practices included a voluntary ban on mortgages that would reduce borrowers' equity and offer borrowers the chance to pay a higher interest rate to avoid prepayment penalties. The Fed was clearly not interested in more regulation and then individuals on Wall Street were mostly concerned about what would happen if they deviated from best practices.

Household debt as a proportion of disposable personal income rose from 80 percent in 1993 to 130 percent in 2006. Over 75 percent of this increase

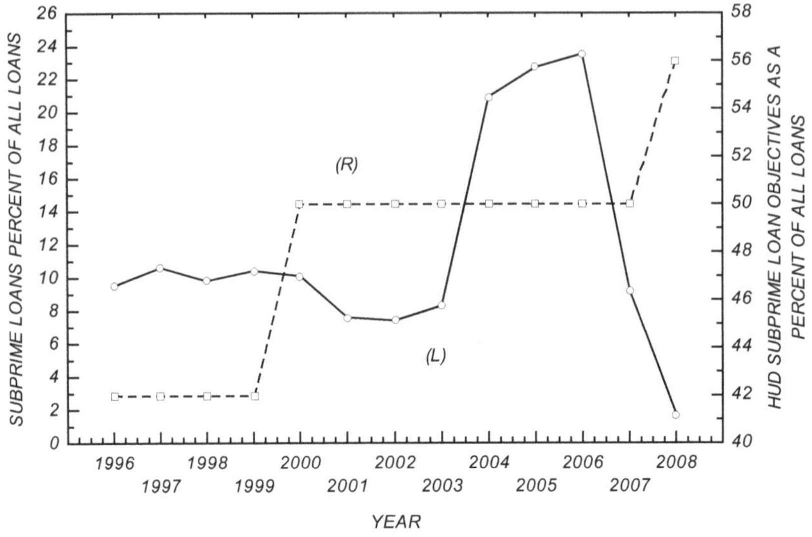

FIGURE 4.4: Percent of Total Loans that were Subprime Compared to HUD Subprime Objectives, 1996-2008

was a result of increases in mortgage debt. In 2000, approximately 9.5 percent of new mortgages were subprime. Following the end of the recession in November 2001, mortgage rates were at a 40-year low (CFCR, 2011, pp. 85) and these lower rates reduced the cost of home ownership. In 2003, credit-worthy borrowers could acquire a thirty-year fixed-rate mortgage for 3 percentage points less than they were able to just three years earlier. Home buyers and home owners used these lower rates as an opportunity to purchase new or used homes, move up to higher priced homes, or obtain home equity loans for desired purchases.

People entered the housing market and prices rose. Florida and California were two of those markets. Homeownership peaked at 69.2 percent of households in 2004. Between the late 1990s and the early 2000s consumer spending rose more rapidly than incomes. Between 1998 and 2005 consumer spending grew from 68 percent to 168 percent of GDP growth. Personal saving declined from 5.2 percent to 1.4 percent. In some years, personal spending grew faster than disposable income.

The subprime mortgage market returned from its adjustment in the late 1990s (see Figure 4.4). In 2003, 93 percent of all subprime loans were made by the top 25 firms. Increasingly larger firms dominated the subprime market.

These firms spent lavishly on subprime lending by acquiring firms, creating new units, or offering financing to mortgage originators. Banks struck out on their own in the securitization market. Investment firms moved into mortgage origination to assure themselves a place in this developing market.

Participants in the subprime process pursued different approaches. Some involved themselves in every step of the mortgaging process. Such companies originated and funded loans, securitized them, and sold the securities to investors. One firm focused on producing a volume of subprime loans. They became the premier firm for this service by creating a specialized production process. For originators who held their mortgage loans, their incentive was to consider all risks in the underwriting process. Those that originated mortgages to sell or distribute began to pay less attention because they suffered no consequences if the loans defaulted (CFCR, 2011, pp. 89). Over half of all mortgages were securitized and distributed before the crisis. More than half of all subprime mortgages were also securitized and distributed.

The mortgage processing system worked to the financial advantage of all participants from the broker to those securitizing and selling securities. The financial returns to the participants acted as an incentive, adding momentum to the process. Brokers relied on up-front fees from the borrower, fees from the lender, or both. They were often involved in finding the best possible interest rates for borrowers. Inflated appraisals were one of the side products of the effort to inflate mortgage prices. Additionally, non-documented loans provided individuals and institutions along the mortgage processing chain with higher yields. Institutions and individuals originating mortgages were pressured into producing mortgages for securitization and they struggled to keep up with demand. No one was being held responsible as these developments continued.

The percentage of mortgages that were subprime peaked in 2006. This peak occurred at the same time that 99 percent of appraisers felt pressure to increase values. The pressure came from mortgage brokers, lenders, real estate agents, and occasionally from borrowers themselves. Failure to raise appraisal amounts often manifests itself in losing a home purchaser. The head of the Fed's consumer subcommittee supported tighter supervision of subprime lenders. This increased supervision would have required an extension of the Fed's authority over independent mortgage companies, state-chartered mortgage companies, parts of banks and thrifts, and bank holding companies. Greenspan did not support instituting more regulation to address predatory lending, so the effort was halted. The examination of subprime institutions did not occur until a pilot was started under Ben Bernanke in July, 2007. Twenty-nine states and Washington DC proceeded to enact legislation to halt predatory lending, establishing 5 percent as an interest rate limit compared to the 8 percent limit at the federal level.

Mortgage loans to low- and moderate-income communities totaled 4.5 trillion dollars in the period from 1977 to 2007. The appropriateness of this amount is a debated matter. According to the FCIC, which presented requests to several large U.S. banks, banks indicated that they had fulfilled most of their promises. The submitted documents indicated that actual commitments to community groups were initially smaller. In addition, the loans issued were not as risky as expected for loans to low-and moderate-income families. The original pledges were not enforced and were never fulfilled.

The boom in housing was supported by the shadow banking system. Money market funds, investors, commercial paper, and repos were the major source of funds. The maintenance of low interest rates by the Fed after the 2001 recession added to the housing boom at an important start-up time. Consumer groups advocated for banks to loan to low- and moderate-income individuals and communities. Banks made commitments, but there was no way of holding them accountable for those commitments.

Risky home mortgage lending was unchecked. The capital that banks required to hold a group of securitized mortgages was less than that which they required to hold whole mortgages. The rating agencies failed those relying on them by prioritizing profit and falsely rating subprime mortgages as triple-A and double-AA. The agencies became part of the credit expansion process, a cog in the mortgage machine. Tranches of securitized loans rated triple-A and super-senior required less capital backing. Lower-level tranches rated A+ and below required higher and higher proportions of capital for support in the case of default. Furthermore, the nationally recognized statistical rating organizations (NRSROs) were regulated once their application had been approved.

For loan origination agencies, volume became more important than quality. Individuals working for these agencies received good salaries, and they were especially rewarded through bonuses. Lending standards decreased as did the level of accountability in the mortgage process. Both individuals and corporate management teams thought prices would continue to escalate and that individuals would continue to buy and invest in real estate.

Subprime mortgages became ubiquitous in the financial system, and risky mortgages were held and sold. The originate-and-distribute method allowed responsibility and accountability to be diffused to the extent it no longer existed. The desire for quick profits motivated the actions of investors and other actors in the mortgage process.

Moving lower level tranches was difficult. Triple-A, and super-senior tranches, which made up approximately 80 percent of those sold, were not difficult to sell because they were associated with higher interest rates and lower default risks. It was not clear to investors that when a mortgage-backed security rated BBB was made into a new security, it was usually rated triple-A. Ratings firms argued that these techniques were justifiable because of the benefits of diversification. These new securities were called credit default obligations (CDOs).

The sources of profit for firms selling CDOs to investors were the difference the CDO paid to investors and the interest the CDO returned on bonds and loans held by the CDO issuer. The participants in the CDO development process obtained liberal profits. However, high levels of risk were involved. The large investment banks continued to engage in risky activities and the SEC failed to require them to have adequate capital and liquidity to support these activities.

Home prices rose by differing amounts in different markets. Average home prices grew by 50 percent in the 5 years prior to and in the first quarter of 2005. The number of homes in rapidly growing markets such as California and Florida doubled during the same time period. The housing market was preparing for a bust. Mortgage fraud was frequent in areas where there was little or no oversight. Fraud data were inadequate. The concern was that fraud would become an epidemic in mortgage markets, thereby threatening their stability.

Credit default obligations were increasingly composed of subprime mortgages. Managers who developed CDOs retained a decreasing proportion of equity in CDOs from 2002 to 2006. ACA Capital is a prime example. In 2002 and 2003, ACA held 100 percent of the equity in the CDOs it originated, whereas that figure was between 0 and 11 percent for deals in 2006 (CFCR, 2011, pp.190).

The pay-as-you go credit default swap (CDS) came into being in June 2006. CDSs were easier to issue and sell because they were similar to actual mortgage-backed securities. The emergence of the CDS fostered a second development; an index was created on the basis of prices of CDSs. This index made it possible to evaluate the performance of the nonprime mortgage market (CFCR, 2011, pp. 190). This index fell as the need for protection increased.

Synthetic CDOs became common. It was easier to create a synthetic portfolio of pay-as-you-go CDOs than to prepare a regular CDO from mortgage-backed securities. Banks moderated much of the risk of synthetic CDOs by retaining the super-senior and triple-A tranches, and by selling tranches below triple-A primarily to other CDOs. Synthetic CDOs were appealing because their equity tranches yielded 7–8 percent more than those of cash CDOs (13 percent) (CFCR, 2011, pp.191).

The new derivatives were designed to allow short-term-investors to bet against the housing boom. Collusion occurred between buyers and sellers.

The investors (buyers) were cooperating with the sellers in choosing collateral. Prices on homes continued to increase. Some wagered that the bubble would burst, while; others continued to invest in housing.

Within banks and investment firms, different units had different levels of exposures to the same CDO. A CDO unit would prepare a given CDO, a different unit would purchase protection for the underlying collateral, and yet another unit would purchase the unfunded super-senior tranche. If there were issues with the CDO's collateral the CDO would pay the unit that purchased credit protection for the collateral. When the CDO ran out of money, it relied on the unit that had the unfunded tranche. Needless to say, managerial understandings of these arrangements were limited (CFCR, 2011, pp.197).

The origination of CDOs continued from 2003 to 2007. Investment firms created new CDOs from old CDOs that were difficult to sell. Some investment firms made buying their own products a practice. From 2003 to 2007, Merrill Lynch sold 142 CDOs and 134 CDOs sold at least one tranche into another Merrill Lynch CDO. Lower tranches that would not sell were subject to a gentleman's agreement: "you buy my BBB tranche and I'll buy yours" (CFCR, 2011, pp. 203). Interest was focused on short-term profit.

Home prices fell in early 2007, particularly in regions of the U.S. that had been booming. An increasing number of borrowers with subprime and ARM mortgages were unable to make their mortgage payments. A small group of important companies assumed much of the risk associated with mortgage-backed securities. These companies had large holdings and were supposedly invested in safe CDOs. However, mortgage defaults and delinquencies increased in 2007. Ratings agencies downgraded mortgage-backed securities and CDOs. Hedge funds, confronted with margin calls, were forced to sell at unprofitable prices, and occasionally had to shut down. The markets for subprime securities, subprime adjustable-rate securities, and CDOs declined quickly (see Table 4.3).

In the third and fourth quarters of 2008 the securitization of auto loans, credit cards, equipment leases, and small business loans practically stopped. U.S. home prices peaked in April 2006. According to the National Realtors Association, existing home sales dropped 9 percent in 2007. In 2008, prices dropped 17 percent. House prices dropped a total of 28 percent in the 2006–2009 period. The levels of decline varied in different areas. For example, housing prices in Sacramento had declined by 50 percent.

The Home Valuation Code of Conduct was passed to reduce the conflicts of interest between appraisers and banks or mortgage lending facilities. Appraisals could no longer be ordered by appraisers or real estate agents (Rosenberg, 2010).

TABLE 4.3: Quarterly Originations in 2007 and 2008 (in billions of $)

	2nd quarter 2007	3rd quarter 2007	4th quarter 2007	All of 2008
Subprime Securitizations	$75		$27	$12
Subprime (Alt-A)	100		13	
CDOs	90		29	5
Collateralized Loan Obligations	All of 2007	$80	$12	

Source: CFCR, 2011, pp.214

Several questions emerge from this review. First, what caused the housing crisis, and how long will it persist? Second, what caused the economic crisis and what does the future hold? Answers to these questions must contain multiple components because many events and circumstances influenced these crises. Underlying the recession and the likely depression to come are the population dynamics and income dynamics of those expected to have income. Table 4.4 indicates the percentages of first-time buyers and the percent of those trading up by age group.

Table 4.4, Figure 4.5, the data they present, and the previous information will be interpreted together. For the purposes of this interpretation, individuals in the 44 and under age group were grouped for consideration as this age group represents those who are most likely to purchase a home as first-time buyers or as move-up buyers in 2008. Age groups 45–54, 55–64, 65–74, and 75 and over were joined because of their lower percentages of first-time buyers and move-up buyers.

In 2006, males with income who were 15–24 years of age represented the smallest group in the population (Figure 2.3); those who were 25–34 represented the third largest group in the population. Those who were 35 to 44 years of age represented the largest population group, but the group was declining in numbers in 2006.

The fourth largest or the third smallest group was those 65 years of age and over. Those 55 to 64 years of age was the fifth largest and the second smallest

TABLE 4.4: Percent of First Time Homebuyers and Percent of Those Who Are Moving Up (2008)*

Age	Household Head Buyers	First-Time Move-up Buyers
Average	33 years	45 years
Under 35	66%	27%
35–44	20	27
45–54	9	22
55–64	3	13
65–74	1	9
75+	1	3

*Data presented from the National Association of Home Builders (NAHB), Housing Economics Section

group in numbers. This was the status of the male population with income in 2006. The figures for females with income are similar.

I hypothesize that low- and moderate-income housing demand peaked in 2005 and 2006 as population trends and the subprime and mortgage lending crisis reached a critical stage. Housing demand among the income-receiving individuals who are 44 years and below had reached its peak. Creating that peak were the here-to-for detailed dynamics that had been developing for some time. Demand for housing has declined significantly since that time. Analysts are perplexed about the continuing decline of the housing market. Figure 4.5 presents a warning for the future. From 2006 on, the number of individuals in the 65 and over age group increases in number at an increasing rate. Given current trends, in 2019, this will be the largest age group in the male and female population with income. The number of individuals (65–65+) continues to increase through 2040. As individuals who are 65 and over ages and die, housing properties will be put on the market. The used home market will expand and will likely crowd-out a significant proportion of the new housing market.

THE CRASH

Bear Stearns was the first Wall Street firm to be rescued by the Federal Reserve (May, 2008). "The Fed guaranteed a large portion of Bear Stearn's

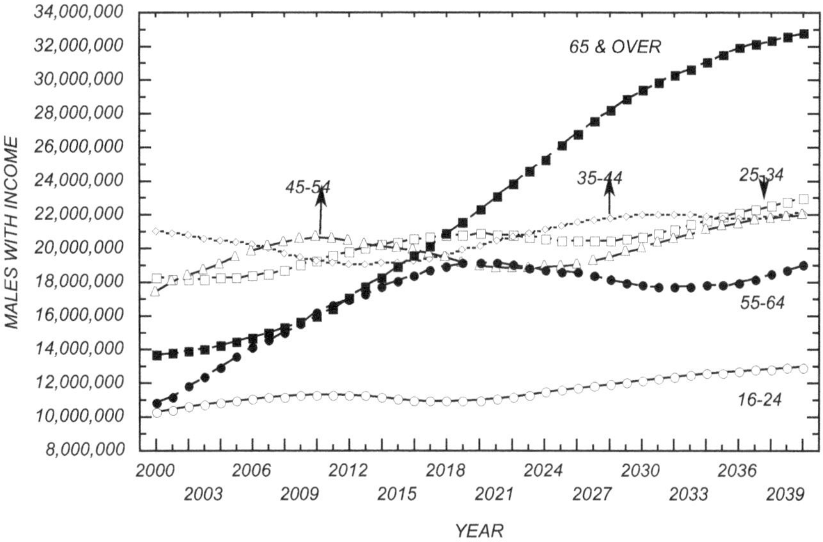

SOURCED: CALCULATIONS FROM BUREAU OF CENSUS AND CURRENT POPULATION SURVEY, ASEC DATA

FIGURE 4.5: White Males with Income by Age, 2000-2040

assets against losses. This was necessary to convince J.P. Morgan to purchase Bear Stearns, which was heavily invested in subprime mortgages and was using risky business practices. The value of Bear Stearns plummeted as investors lost confidence (Rosenberg, 2010).

Lehman Brothers experienced losses of 2.8 billion dollars in the second quarter of 2008. On September fifteenth of that year Lehman filed for bankruptcy. Lehman had 600 billion dollars of assets financed with 60 billion dollars of capital. Bidders for Lehman Brothers wanted government support. Because the U.S. government failed to do so, Lehman failed. Eventually, Barclay's Bank of Britain negotiated an agreement to purchase Lehman out of bankruptcy (Rosenberg, 2010).

Merrill Lynch also struggled for survival. Merrill Lynch lost 1.96 billion dollars on 6.6 billion dollars in write-downs. The record numbers of subprime lenders began declining as homeowners defaulted. Merrill's losses were so large that the Bank of America (BOA) had to increase its borrowing from the U.S. by 20 billion dollars to 45 billion dollars to acquire Merrill (Rosenberg, 2010).

Citigroup, a financial services firm, wrote-down its assets by 18.1 billion dollars in January 2008. Of that amount, 10 billion dollars related to the subprime-mortgage crisis. To survive, Citigroup stopped dividends for three years and cut their workforce by 75,000 individuals. Restrictions on executive salaries were imposed. The U.S. government offered approximately 20 billion dollars to the bank and backed approximately 306 billion dollars in loans and securities Rosenberg, (2010). Losses were divided among the government, Citigroup, the Treasury Department, the Federal Deposit Insurance Company (FDIC), and the Federal Reserve. Citigroup was forced to increase its borrowing from the U.S. by 20 billion dollars bringing their total to 45 billion dollars. The remaining losses were split between Citigroup (10 percent) and the U.S. government (90 percent) (Rosenberg, 2010). In February 2009 the U.S. Treasury Department increased its ownership from 8 percent to 36 percent. Eventually, in July 2009, Citigroup announced quarterly profits of 4.3 billion dollars (Rosenberg, 2010).

Goldman Sachs became a deposit-taking holding company in September 2008. This change made it possible for Goldman to borrow from the Fed. Goldman had a record of profitability extending back to the Great Depression, however, the 2008 crash ended that record. In December 2008, shares of Goldman were down 70 percent. Goldman received 10 billion dollars from the federal government through the Troubled Asset Relief Program (TARP). Goldman was determined to repay government loans with interest as soon as possible. Improved revenues and profits in 2009 enabled the distribution of improved pay packages. Reacting to public outcry regarding pay to senior managers, the top thirty executives were paid stock bonuses that could not be sold for five years (Rosenberg, 2010).

In December 2008, Morgan Stanley reported quarterly losses of 2.36 billion dollars. Nevertheless, Morgan Stanley also reported positive earnings of 1.59 billion dollars per year. In the next quarter Morgan Stanley announced its third quarterly loss in a row. Morgan Stanley had issued a warrant of 950 million dollars to the federal government and it agreed to purchase that warrant back.

The American International Group (AIG) announced that it had lost 7.8 billion dollars in the first quarter of 2008. The U.S. government established an 85 billion dollar line of emergency credit for AIG. This amount was then increased by 38 billion dollars in September 2008. As the world's largest insurance company, it had over 375 million policy holders in the U.S. AIG continued to lose money in August in response to the housing crisis. The U.S. Treasury Department continued to extend loans to AIG and AIG continued to experience losses until the U.S. government eventually owned 80 percent of AIG (Rosenberg, 2010).

President-elect Obama suggested a federal stimulus program to revive a weak economy. In budget reconciliation talks, the House and the Senate agreed to a 787.2 billion dollar package. The American Recovery and

Reinvestment Act (2009) (ARRA) provided for 507 billion dollars in spending programs with a scaled-back version of the middle-class tax relief proposal. Eight-hundred dollars were given to families within identified income limits, 400 dollars for individuals, and a one-time payment of 250 dollars for recipients of Social Security and disability (Rosenberg, 2010).

Thirty-million dollars were allocated to upgrades to the electric grid, the manufacturing of advanced battery technology, and grants for energy efficiency. Doctors, hospitals, and medical centers were able to apply for grants to improve computerized medical information systems. The National Institutes of Health received grants of 8.5 million dollars for disease research. Home weatherization grants in the amount of 5 billion dollars were made available to low- and middle- income families. In addition, 6.3 billion dollars was allocated to energy efficiency upgrades. Road and bridge infrastructure construction projects received 29 billion dollars. Public transit improvement projects and infrastructure investment projects received 8.4 billion dollars. High-speed rail projects received 8 billion dollars. Eighteen-billion dollars was set aside for environmental cleanup, flood prevention, and water infrastructure projects.

School aid in the amount of 40.6 billion dollars was sent to local school districts to balance school budgets, prevent cutbacks, and modernize schools. The temporary increase in Medicaid funding for states amounted to 87 billion dollars. Eight billion dollars were allocated to states for public safety and critical services. Fourteen billion dollars were set aside for an education tax credit for tuition and book expenses. In a boost to college and graduate education, Pell Grants were increased from 5,350 to 5,550 dollars annually. Two-hundred billion dollars was allocated to work-study programs. Jobless benefits were increased by 257 billion dollars; some were extended twenty weeks in addition to regular unemployment compensation (UC); in 29 states with high unemployment rates an additional thirty-three weeks were added. Two billion in funds were allocated for purchasing and rehabilitating vacant and foreclosed properties.

The ARRA legislation gave states 150 billion dollars over a period of 2.5 years. Despite this significant funding state deficits remain. The same is true at the federal level.

General Motors experienced losses of 30.9 billion dollars in 2008. Auto sales declined 11 percent internationally and in the U.S., GM borrowed almost two-thirds of this money from the U.S. GM annual sales are presented below:

In response to its declining market share GM found purchasers for its Hummer and Saturn brands, sold its Saab unit to a Swedish maker, and cut 6,000 salaried jobs and 34 percent of executive jobs. GM returned to the

TABLE 4.5: Proportion of U.S. Car Sales by GM in Specified Years*

Year	Market Share
1980	45%
1990	35
2000	28
(June) 2009	19

*Source: The Concise Encyclopedia of the Great Recession

auto-leasing market in August 2009. Twenty-two percent of GM's new-car sales were leases. GM's global sales picture was mixed. China provided approximately 25 percent of all sales. That figure grew to a projected 40 percent in 2009. In November 2009, GM began to pay back 6.7 billion dollars in loans at a rate of one billion dollars a quarter to the U.S. government and 200 million dollars per quarter to the Canadian government. In November of 2009, GM reported losses of 1.15 million dollar. Revenue had fallen by 28 billion dollars from a similar period in 2008. Eventually, GM was able to repay its debt to the federal government.

Chrysler and GM entered bankruptcy in late April 2008 and June 1, 2008 respectively. Chrysler arrived at an agreement with Fiat on June 10, 2008. The bailouts of GM and Chrysler cost taxpayers more than 29.12 billion dollars. Industry-wide car sales continued to decline. Car- and truck- manufacturers were using approximately 65 percent of their productive capacity. World-wide capacity utilization is expected to reach 85 percent by 2015 (Rosenberg, 2010).

The Troubled Asset Relief Plan (TARP) (October 27, 2008) was started when the U.S. dispersed 125 billion dollars to ensure that credit would flow again. This sum was a small portion of the 700 billion dollars designated for this purpose. The Department of the Treasury had committed all but 60 billion dollars of the total amount by November 2008. Bank of America (BOA) played an essential part in the U.S. recovery. In January 2008, BOA purchased Countrywide Financial for 4 billion dollars. In addition to the purchase of Merrill Lynch for 19.36 billion dollars, this made BOA the right to claim it was the nation's largest bank with 2.7 trillion dollars on its books.

The housing crisis and the challenges that banks experienced during this period were responsible for the widespread liquidation of assets by individuals. These individuals could not get enough credit to sustain them through the bankruptcy process. Consumer filings totaled 1,064,927 in 2008, up from 801,840 in 2007 (Rosenberg, 2010).

At the stock market's peak, the market capitalization of the 29 largest financial firms was 1.86 trillion dollars. This concentration of wealth and capital increased the possibility of failure and complicated the process of recovery. One year after Lehman filed for bankruptcy, seven of the larger financial firms disappeared; only twenty-two firms remained to be traded in September 2009.

In November 2009, five million households (1 in 10) were estimated to be one month behind on their mortgage payments. The federal government offered mortgage notes to struggling homeowners at lower interest rates and enrolled them in payback programs. Start-ups are assumed to be critical to economic recoveries as effective demand increases and declines. The effective demand of an economy determines the health of an economy. New housing sales and sales of used housing peaked because of overbuilding and lack of demand. Subprime housing mortgages were foreclosed because of poor practices throughout the mortgage, lending, and investment processes.

In January 2008, OPEC (Organization of Economic Cooperation and Development) could not control rising oil prices. In December 2009 the price of oil exceeded 147 dollars per barrel. In April and May 2010, oil prices increased above 4.10 dollars per gallon. At this level, demand began to decline.

Part of the problem associated with relying on individuals to regulate the financial industry is that they are often selected come from the industry they are selected to regulate. This is justified by claims that regulators must know about the institutions they are trying to regulate. In addition, to the old-boy-network, the pay czar of the U.S. Department of the Treasury had the power to place limits on the pay offered by Wall Street firms and federal firms.

DISPOSABLE PERSONAL INCOME

Three quantities: total personal income (PI), total personal consumption (PC), and total disposable personal income (DPI) were estimated. The personal income estimate was made and presented in Chapter 1 and 2. The results of the personal disposable income estimate are presented in Figure 4.6 from 2000 to 2040.

Disposable personal income is defined using the following formula (4.1):

$$DPI_{gt} = \sum_{g=1}^{g=n} \bar{N}_{gt} (\bar{PI}_{gt} - \bar{tx}_{gt} \pm \bar{db}_{gt} \pm \bar{sv}_{gt}) \quad (4.1)$$

DPI_{gt} = average personal disposable income of group g at time t

$\bar{tx}_{gt}$ = average taxes of group g at time t

$\bar{db}_{gt}$ = average debt for group g at time t

$\bar{sv}_{gt}$ = average savings for group g at time t

N_{gt} = number in group g at time t

As Figure 4.6 indicates, the estimated DPI for the year 2000 is 7.629 trillion dollars. In this projection, DPI is expected to increase to an inflection point in 2021–2022 reaching 16.015 trillion dollars in 2021 and; 16.231 trillion dollars in 2022. The increase continues in an approximately straight line to an estimated DPI of 220.039 trillion dollars in 2040. The average annual rate of increase from 2000 to 2040 is 311.35 billion dollars.

The line scaled according to the right axis, presents the annual percentage rate of DPI change in U.S. The general trend in the percentage rate of change in estimated DPI from 2000 to 2033 is decreasing. From 2000 to 2003, the annual estimated percent change of DPI dips from 5.15 percent to 4.75 percent. The estimated percent change in DPI reaches a minor peak of 4.99 percent in 2005. From 2005–2006, the annual percentage change declines to 0.90 percent in 2033 and 0.86 percent in 2035. In 2006, the percentage change increases slightly by an estimated 1.55 percent. In 2036, the annual estimated percent change was .99 percent. The estimated DPI percentage change then increased to 1.13 percent in 2040.

What conclusions can be drawn from this data? Initially, DPI is correlated with the annual percent change in DPI, with $r = -.98$, $p = 0.00$, $N = 40$. This result can be expected given that the latter variable is derivative of the former variable. The estimated DPI increase occurs at a declining rate of increase. This rate of increase must exceed the rate of inflation for actual DPI to remain positive (Table 4.6). Additionally, the actual rate of increase in total personal income must be above the rate of increase in 2008 dollars. A

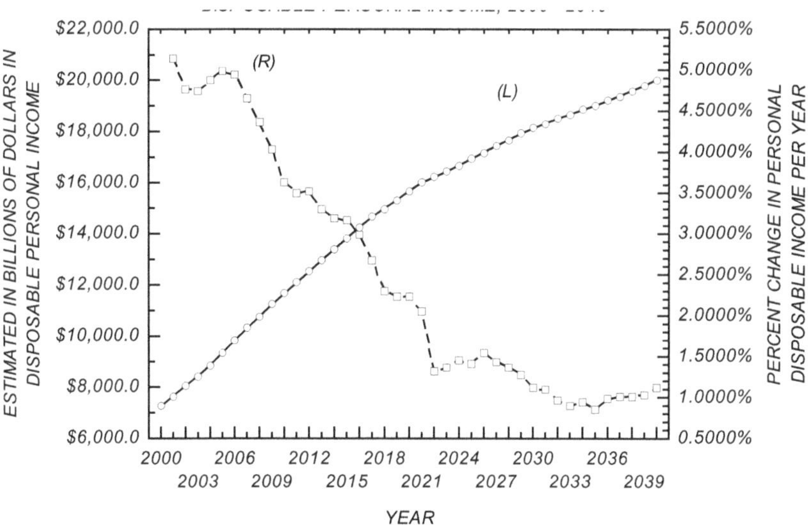

SOURCE: CALCULATIONS FROM CURRENT POPULATION SURVEY DATA, ASEC DATA, NIPA DATA, AND SOCIAL SECURITY DATA

FIGURE 4.6: Estimated Disposable Personal Income, and Annual Change in Disposable Personal Income, 2000-2040

decline to a level below that of the 2008 dollar could lead to declining levels of disposable personal income.

Table 4.6 compares the actual rate of increase in DPI as indicated by the Bureau of Labor Statistics, NIPA data to the estimated annual rate of change in DPI.

These data are based on equations in which estimated personal income as derived from the Current Population Survey, Annual Social and Economic Supplement (ASEC), 1967–2011. Estimated personal income is used as an independent variable and actual disposable personal income, as derived from (NIPA) tables from the Bureau of Labor Statistics. This variable is used as a dependent variable.

Table 4.6 presents data indicating that the actual annual percent change in DPI listed in the NIPA tables (Bureau of Labor Statistics) is a fraction of one percent different from the values for the estimated DPI for the 2001–2010 period. Furthermore, the difference between the values for the actual DPI percentage change and the estimated DPI change declines from 2001 to 2010. The estimated DPI annual change values decline to less than 1 from 2032 to 2036 and decline from 2001 to 2033.

TABLE 4.6: Changes in DPI: Actual, Estimated, and Percent Difference*

Year	(Col. 1) Actual DPI Percent Annual Change	(Col. 2) Estimated DPI; Percent Annual Change (NIPA)	(Col. 1 – Col. 2) Difference in Percent Change
2001	5.4%	5.15%	.28%
2002	5.0	4.78	.24
2003	5.0	4.75	.24
2004	5.1	4.89	.25
2005	5.3	4.99	.26
2006	5.2	4.95	.26
2007	4.9	4.65	.23
2008	4.6	4.37	.20
2009	4.2	4.04	.17
2010	3.8	3.64	.16

* some differences due to rounding

CONCLUSIONS

- The saturation of effective demand was the basic cause of the housing bust. The factors contributing to that were subprime loans, changing mortgage lending standards and practices, securitization, and increasing HUD standards for low and moderate-income housing sales.
- From 2002 to 2006, the value of securitized loans grew to a peak of 450 billion dollars.
- Fannie Mae, Freddie Mac, and investment firms created demand for mortgages that resulted in a saturated housing market in 2007–2008. During this time, housing construction outstripped demand in the U.S.
- The failure of the Federal Reserve to regulate the mortgage lending process or to raise interest rates was a factor in the housing boom and bust. Unethical behavior, a lack of regulation throughout the housing system, a decline in mortgage standards, and practices that either bordered on illegal or were illegal, plagued the system.
- The abuse of securitization practices was a major contributor to the weakening of the financial system.

- HUD's increasing low- to moderate-income mortgage quotas led Fannie and Freddie to lower their mortgage lending standards.
- The SEC generally failed to regulate investment firms and the securitization process.
- The estimates for DPI from 2000 to 2040 indicate an increasing annual DPI with a decreasing annual percentage rate of change from 2006 to 2033 and in 2035.
- If these estimates, in 2008 dollars, are correct within a relatively small (.25 percent to .16 percent) margin of error there are a number of implications for the U.S. economy.

1. The unemployment rate will vary. Several factors will contribute to this variation. First, a large number of people will be 65 and over during the period from 2012 to 2040. This will reduce the size of the civilian labor force, the denominator in the unemployment rate, in the U.S. The numerator will decline by 1 for every 64 year old that becomes 65, (excluding those who continue to be or are newly employed).
2. The relatively straight lines on the graph in Figure 4.5 from 2000 to 2040 in the 16–24, 25–34, 35–44, and 45–54 age ranges will contribute steadily to DPI.
3. As individuals with incomes move into the 65+ age category the rate of retirement will increase and average salaries for males with income will decrease. The average DPI and the total change in DPI for this age and sex group will depend on the number in the group and the group's annual average income. This same is true for females. This will affect the annual rate of change in DPI.
4. A decline in income for individuals in the age range from 55–64 during the period from 2023 to 2033 will decrease the DPI for that group. This will affect the annual rate of change in DPI.
5. Items 1–4 partially explain the decline in the annual rate of DPI change seen in Figure 4.6.
6. Estimates of personal income are based on individuals with income grouped by sex and age group (Current Population Survey, Annual Social and Economic Supplement 1967–2000, 1967–2011). The results from these estimates were tested using estimated personal income as an independent variable and NIPA variables for personal income (PI) and disposable personal income (DPI) as the dependent variables. Koo (2008) was mistaken in suggesting recessions are balance sheet recessions. Recessions and depressions begin with a lack of effective demand and are preceded and accompanied by related changes in a country's

financial and economic systems. The attempts of businesses in adjusting their balance sheets during economic hard times are to adjust to a lack of demand for their products and services.

7. The relationship between population and DPI depends on the sex, the numbers in a group with income, and the average income for each group. This can be refined further.
8. Ensuring access to capital by maintaining low interest rates is not a substitute for increasing effective demand, which is essential to economic improvement.

CHAPTER 5

Demographics, Personal Income, and Economic Asymmetry

INTRODUCTION

Algorithms are presented for understanding economic stress, aggregate and disaggregated demand and supply, personal income, personal consumption, demographic change, business, and employment. A method of categorizing economic shocks is proposed. Equations are presented which demonstrate the influence of demographic variables on personal income. The effects of population change on aggregated demand are presented. The algorithm for the calculation of subgroup personal income is applied to data for a single ethnic subgroup. Figures are used to demonstrate the calculation process for total personal income. The results provide insight into one source of the current economic slowdown in the United States.

Background

While there was much early concern about economic asymmetry and its sources (Holly and Stannett 2002, and Stannett 2002), the empirical study of economic asymmetries was most thoroughly engaged in by Wesley Mitchell (1913, 1951, and 1961). Mitchell established many of the issues that are central to the discussion of business cycles and economic asymmetry today. One of those forces that Mitchell introduced is that of economic shocks. The theory of shocks, which has a prominent place in the explanation of specific periods of variation in the economy, is a theoretical framework that admits to the occurrence of special circumstances as a source of economic variation. Thus, dramatic price changes in supplies such as oil, war, major weather or other natural events influencing crop production, high levels of bankruptcy, bank insolvency, and rapid dislocations or advances created by changing technology are examples of shocks. What is of importance about the asymmetries introduced by shocks is that each shock has its own special cause. The lack of a general cause makes the establishment of general theory for this type of economic asymmetry difficult.

Mitchell (1913, 1951, and 1961) was an indefatigable chronicler of movement in the cycles of a myriad of indicators of business, labor, financial, imports, exports, prices, and other statistics. He did all of this in search for a general understanding of the reasons for business cycles. In monitoring the expansion, peak, contraction, and trough phases of thirty-four series monitoring business cycles he was able to develop observations related to the segments of business cycles. Mitchell (1951) suggested there is, in every segment of the economy, changes in average reference-cycle standings show greater concentration of movements in an upward (expansion) or downward (contraction) direction than do the observations of individual cycles. Furthermore, he suggested that the variation tends to be greater at the beginning of periods of decline and at the beginnings of periods of expansion. In his 1961 research, Mitchell observed that the transformation of business cycle data has a long practice. He suggested that the search for explanation of business cycle is most likely to be successful if guided by rational hypotheses. These efforts to identify rational hypotheses resulted in the accumulation of a great deal of time series data. However, many of the data series collected varied in a non-homogenous manner and defied generalized interpretations.

Mitchell (1951), in summarizing, suggests that the net result of random forces acting in any given part of a business cycle may be weak or strong depending on the related cyclical influences. As these influences remain unidentified, Mitchell, with his customary empirical rigor, suggests, "even now what we can say is ill proportioned, tentative, and subject to change as investigation proceeds" (p. 5, 1951).

Inflation is another source of economic asymmetry. Variation in the price of commodities, goods, and services can occur in either direction. Deflation in the United States (Friedman and Schwartz, 1963) occurred in the United States during the Depression years. While empirically this has never been adequately explained, the decomposed aggregate demand and aggregate supply framework may provide some tentative hypotheses (see Table 5.2) about this time. One would suspect that such times feature lack of demand or excess supply. A time of strategic importance for inflation occurred in the 1970's (Feldstein 1991). An excessively easy monetary policy from the middle to the late 1970's was accompanied by low, but increasing interest rates. Inflation levels increased until 1979 when the United States Federal Reserve Bank moved interest rates higher to stymie investment. The high levels of inflation in the latter years of the Carter administration (1979–1982) threatened to disrupt the United States economy. The savings and loan crisis occurred primarily because of the rapid inflation of the 1970's. Interest rates to depositors rose significantly while loans held by institutions were primarily fixed-rate mortgages. The market value of mortgages held by thrift institutions fell so they were worth less than the value of thrift deposits and other obligations.

This is a common perception of inflation that may be related to a second consideration. Another source of inflation is highlighted by Irving Fisher (1928) in his discussion of the "money illusion." He shows that perceptions in the high cost of living due to the rise in price of commodities can be a result of variation in the value of the money unit itself. Money is pegged to a certain value or allowed to float in value with the anticipation of creating a basis for stable currency value. This source of economic asymmetry has repeated itself with serious consequences for the economies involved.

What cannot be doubted is the important role that money has played in economic crises both in the United States and internationally. Periods of hyperinflation Austria (1919–1922), Hungary (1942–1946), Germany (1917–1923, 1932–1944), Greece (1938–1944), Poland (1921–1924), and Russia (1922–1924) documented by Cagan (1956); and Germany (1938–1944) (Klein 1956) are examples of what happens when the money supply is excessive.

Friedman and Schwartz (1963, 1982) in their surveys of the history of money in the United States and England make a case for the primacy of money in business cycles and economic change. Their review of the Depression highlights issues they consider central to the maintenance of economic stability. They perceive that positive growth in the economy is maintained by a modest, but regular growth in the money supply. The money supply equation presented by Friedman (1956) contains the following terms and maintains a term (u) that stands for unexplained tastes and preferences.

Additional, but related theories of economic shock and asymmetry are those of over-production and under-consumption. These related economic concepts are important relationships. These possibilities are dealt with directly in a part of the theoretical work presented herein. Whenever issues of over-production and under-consumption are discussed, the issues of supply-price, supply-quantity, demand-price, and demand-quantity must be discussed concurrently.

The presence of excess inventories in an economy or one of its sectors may be a witness to the presence of over-production or imperfect information. There is the alternative perspective that the availability of excess inventories is a consequence of under-consumption. In the classical view, production of goods is its own source of consumption as production creates the wealth for consumption. Currently it is well understood that there are income distribution issues involved in the production of goods and services that make for unevenness in consumption between individuals. The presence of malnutrition is an example of the presence of under-consumption in this revised view of the nature of under-consumption. Asymmetries in production and consumption exist at international, national, and sub-national levels. When investment is made in the production of goods for which there is no market there are economic asymmetries. These asymmetries occur for specific businesses or within specific sectors of the economy. Recent overproduction (or declining demand) in the housing sector of the United States economy offers a prescient example of the lack of effective demand.

Structural factors in national economies and the international economic framework may create sources of asymmetry. Private, national, as well as international economic arrangements may create significant barriers to coordinating levels of supply and demand. The multiplicity of national and private economic actors makes economic imbalance and asymmetries at disaggregated and aggregated levels inevitable.

Easterlin (1965) summarizes findings on the nature of long swings or Kuznets cycles of population and labor force growth in the United States. Cross-sectional data series were used, some from the pre-World War I period, but with some series extending to 1950. Many series are from decennial population censuses of 1870 to 1950. Early in this period (until 1920), swings were largely related to immigration. Up to 1950 fertility assumed a more important role. White native-born population shows conformity to long swings throughout the entire period. After 1920, the African-American component also shows conformity to the long swings in the labor force. Long swings in output growth typically appear to precede those in the rate of immigration. Evidence points to United States demand conditions as the *systematic* factor resulting in migration swings. This culminates in the tentative conclusion that immigration appears to be a result of swings in the rate of economic growth, although such movement may well have played an important functional role.

Summarizing (Easterlin 1965), up to 1914, long swings of population and labor force of fifteen to twenty-five years were observed. A speculative interpretation of the swings was presented. A sequence of prior swings in the rate of economic growth, and rise in aggregate demand associated with business investment was accompanied by a growth rate of wage rates and a decline in unemployment. Migration from farm areas to urban centers and from abroad then ensues. During contractions, the same sequence tended to prevail in reverse. From 1914 to 1950, long swings in labor force and population growth have continued, but have demonstrated different characteristics. The birth rate assumes a much greater role in the swings. Easterlin (1965) raises significant questions about the interpretation of these long swings, noting the need to develop a meaningful analytical model that is consistent with these observations.

To supply information on the empirical associations between migration, United States population, United States live births, civilian labor force, gross domestic product, and the unemployment rate a series of correlations were prepared. For the results see the correlation matrix in Table 5.1.

The study of growth as developed by Solow (1970, 1988) is important for its understanding of the combined influence of the dependence of growth rates of output on those of labor and capital. The rate of growth of output is stated in Box 5.2. The reformulation of this equation suggests that the interaction of labor and the other terms in the equation play an important role in economic growth. This term is called multifactor productivity growth, or the Solow residual.

The rate of growth of output per man-hour is related positively to the rate of growth of the capital-output ratio and positively to the multifactor

TABLE 5.1: Correlations of Macroeconomic, Long Term Variables (N=77), 1929-2006

	USPOP	CLF	GDP	IMMIG	BIRTHS	UNEMP	PI
CLF	.974**	---					
GDP	.977**	.993**	---				
IMMIG	.827**	.855**	.847**	---			
BIRTHS	.607**	.51**	.535**	.527**	----		
UNEMP	-.360*	-.260*	-.326*	-.263*	-.677**	---	
PI	.975**	.996**	.999	.849**	.555**	-.296*	---
PC	.972**	.995**	.998	.851**	.554**	-.281*	.999**

*Significant at p<.05; **Significant at p<.001

Sources: National Income and Product Accounts, U.S. Department of Commerce; U.S. Department of Labor; National Center for Health Statistics

DEFINITIONS FOR TABLE 5.1

USPOP—United States population	CLF—civilian labor force
GDP—gross domestic product	IMMIG—immigration
BIRTHS—live births	UNEMP—unemployment rate
PI—personal income	PC—personal consumption

productivity growth term. From 1874 through 1986, there has been a relatively constant output-capital ratio. This means that the Solow residual has been approximately equal to the share of labor multiplied by the growth rate of labor productivity. During the 1874–1986 period, multifactor productivity (Solow residual) accounts for over half the growth in the private economy. The research problem remaining is that there is only limited understanding of the source(s) of this residual. Also remaining is the need to find adequate explanations of how the stochastic variations characterized by changing unemployment and periods of expansion and decline in output occur.

SOLOW OUTPUT FUNCTION

$$g_y = ag_n + (1-a)g_k + q \quad (5.2)$$

g_y =output a = share of labor in output
g_n = growth rate of labor, g_k = growth rate of capital
q = that part of growth that is unexplained by the other variables

Simon Kuznets (1966, 1973) further advances the role of population in economic growth by analyzing the historical role of population increase and growth in per capita product as mutually occurring events in developed economies (1966, pp. 20). Using data from 12 developed nations for the 1954–1960 period, Kuznets finds the share of gross national product that is personal income to be approximately 88 percent. He also suggests that as economic growth occurs, the share of personal income in total output may be changing. Kuznets compares data on the share of labor in national income between 1909–1913 and 1954–1958. He observes, "The price per man-hour relative to the price per service unit of capital had to rise by the difference between 2.84 and .87 percent per year." This is a price differential of 2.41 times between the two periods.

Denison (1962, 1974) provides evidence on the reasons the price per man-hour of labor has increased at a faster rate than the price per unit of capital services. He classifies these as improvements in the "quality of labor." He suggests that improvements in educational levels account for approximately .78 percent per year compared to a growth in total man-hours of labor of .87 percent per year. Other sources of change were growth in the efficiency of labor (associated with a reduction in working hours) of .43 percent per year and increased efficiency of female labor (.14 percent). These changes have resulted in an increase in the growth of labor input (in terms of man-hours) from .87 to 2.22 percent per year.

National income is divided between labor and capital. Kuznets (1966) emphasizes that it is "*live* labor" that has brought about improvements in the proportion of labor as a part of national income. His estimates and those based on Denison's work (1962) result in the labor share of national income in the United States being 76.9 percent compared to an actual measured share of 77.3 percent. It is concluded that the share of labor as a portion of net output had increased in recent decades because of the increased investment in maintaining and improving the quality of labor.

Denison's (1962) work emphasizes the estimation of the influence of several factors such as education of the work force, length of workday, spread of knowledge, economies of scale, and sex of worker to understand the growth of product attributable to each factor.

A second approach enlarges the scope of the term capital beyond material stocks to include investment in the education of human beings through formal means or by on-the-job training and experience. This approach was developed by Schultz (1960) and Becker (1975). How does the quality of labor and its educational level factor into understanding economic asymmetry, if it does at all?

Kuznets suggests there is a residual (*unexplained*) efficiency of growth of output per unit of total input that amounted to approximately a third of the rate of growth in total input for the 1909–1957 period.

These gains in "residual efficiency" are components of the increase in total output *not* accounted for by sources of measured inputs. The question stands out. Why this large component of national income due to "residual efficiency"? Is this residual efficiency in any way related to issues of economic asymmetry and/or demographic change?

Kuznets (1966) also notes the trends in the distribution in the labor force in six nations over differing periods of time. These trends indicate significant increases in the proportions of individuals in employee status as compared to those who were entrepreneurs and self-employed. Additional changes in occupational status have been accompanied by changes in shifts in sex distribution of employees. In Table 4.4 (p. 192) Kuznets presents these changing distributions over the 1900 to 1960 period. Can these demographic factors, or others be related to issues of economic asymmetry?

Kuznets (1973) analyzing the relationship of population growth and *per capita* income for 21 developed nations from the early 1950's to 1964 finds a negative Spearman correlation of $r = -.434$. However, when taking out four countries that had populations with higher growth rates than those of Europe and Japan, the Spearman correlation became $r = .061$. Kuznets quantitative efforts are limited, however, by lack of data necessary to cover important structural divisions in the economy. He suggests (1973):

> Both the effects of population increase on aspects of economic growth other than aggregate income per capita and the differential impact of population growth on distinct economic groups within a country obviously merit further analysis (p. 48).

This is followed by an observation very relevant to this research: the number of consumer equivalent units is altered by changing levels of population growth (pp.14–15).

Kuznets (1973) follows this by stating "material capital stock effectively increases output *only* if it is supplemented by some uses of product now classified as *consumption*" (p.25) (emphasis mine). This statement emphasizes the importance of consumption to the growth of the output of capital stock. It is indicative of a relationship that is causal in the direction from increased consumption to the increase in the output from material capital stock. Thus it is important to define the constraints on consumption assume a primary role in economic change and growth.

The next step in understanding the nature of economic asymmetry is aided by finding an aggregate economic measure that varies directly or in a similar way, as do business cycles. Business cycles are the economic manifestation of economic asymmetry. As such having a measure that varies in a parallel manner will offer a possible approach to modeling or explaining economic asymmetry. Daniel Creamer's (1956) study of personal income during business cycles provides a longitudinal time series for personal income in the United States that is compared to the peaks and troughs of business cycles over the 1909–1951 periods. In summarizing Creamer (1956) maintains that despite long-term shifts in proprietary, labor, and property income, "there is a one-to-one correspondence of personal income cycles and business cycles." He observes that the turning points in personal income may be measured in current or constant prices with the exception of period of war, its aftermath or periods of rapidly changing prices.

The use of personal income as an explanatory variable for periods of economic asymmetry is reinforced by existing practices of the National Bureau of Economic Research. The National Bureau of Economic Research (NBER) uses four primary indicators of economic activity to delineate the peaks, duration, and troughs of business cycles (National Bureau of Economic Research, 2002). Economy wide employment, industrial production, real personal income (minus transfer payments) and wholesale-retail sales are outlined as the most important NBER indicators in estimating business cycles. A recession begins just after the economy reaches a peak of activity and ends as the economy reaches its trough. Between the trough and the peak the economy is in an expansion. A recession is defined as "a significant decline in activity across the economy, lasting more than a few months, visible in industrial production, employment, real personal income (minus transfer payments), and wholesale-retail sales."

The value of these indicators to the later theoretical and applied developments will become clear.

Different theorists perceive the constraints on personal income in different ways. Keynes (1936) set forth a relatively stable relationship between income, consumption, and savings. He saw consumers as having relatively strong habits and as such changes in the propensity to consume were likely to adjust slowly. Keynes saw short-term changes in consumption to be depended primarily on short-term changes in wage-units. Keynes added that as a general rule as income increased, the proportion of income saved increases. The Keynesian consumption function makes possible a characterization of the relationship between disposable income and consumption expenditures.

Keynesian theory (1936) concerned itself with the ability of a market system to maintain full employment and its related stability. Important to his formulation was the ability of an economy to maintain "effective demand." The level of effective demand is determined in the context of population constraints and level of technological advancement.

Whereas monetarists and quantity of money theorists are concerned with the money supply and its impact on prices, Keynes was interested in the conditions that affected output levels. He was concerned about the conditions that determined the level of employment in an economy. Keynes maintained the level of employment determined the level of "effective" (or aggregate) demand. In these terms, the Keynesian perspective would maintain there is a steady relationship between aggregate personal consumption expenditures and aggregate personal income. This relationship is known as the Absolute Income Hypothesis. Therefore, he argued that decreases or cuts in wages would result in declining demand, thereby increasing unemployment. A general statement of a Keynesian consumption function is in Box 5.3 (Ruby 2002).

CONSUMPTION FUNCTION

$C = a + bY_d$ where (5.3)

C = consumption expenditures

a = consumption expenditure independent of the level of income

b = the marginal propensity to consume

Y_d = current disposable income

The level of aggregate demand was primarily dependent on the level of investment in the economy. If there is no method of determining the correct level of investment in an economy and adjusting to that level there will not be full employment.

Ferber (1953) suggests that the adjustment of consumption functions for population "would seem to constitute a basic criterion of a valid aggregate (consumption) function" (p. 12). In his classification and review of twenty-four consumption functions, twelve made no adjustment for population. He draws attention to the work of Staehle (1937) who suggests in the Keynesian view, consumption will adjust to the level of income. The level of employment determines the level of income. Levels of investment determine the level of employment. Keynes argued that the that the degree of inequality in the *distribution of labor income approximates the importance of the amount of labor income in wage units* (emphasis mine) in explaining the fluctuations in the ratio of retail sales to labor income. This suggestion is central to the theoretical and empirical work necessary to understand important aspects of economic asymmetry.

A significant departure from the Keynesian consumption function occurred with the development of the permanent-income hypothesis (Friedman, 1957). The permanent-income hypothesis maintains that the consumption of the household or individual depends on its (or his/her) expectation of income and wealth to be derived over a lifetime. In this view, the individual holds his wealth intact while consuming a relatively constant proportion of the present value of income flowing from work and wealth holdings. Measured income and measured consumption are made of permanent and transitory components. The permanent elements are the planned and anticipated elements of consumption. The transitory elements are gains of losses of income and unanticipated changes in consumption. Individuals will consume a constant proportion of their permanent income over the long-run. A significant proportion of households/individuals will experience a declining component of income over the business cycle that will result in an increase in their average propensity to consume. This set of conditions gives rise to the short-run consumption function.

With this approach, there are significant issues related to the estimation of values for permanent income and consumption. The purchase of consumer durables is distinguished as investment by the individual/household, while only the flow of services from the purchase of durables is counted as consumption. This and distinguishing between permanent and transitory income represent complex measurement issues.

Another variant of the permanent-income hypothesis is the life-cycle hypothesis presented by Modigliani and Brumberg (1954). The life-cycle theory assumes the individual consumes a constant proportion of the present value of their lifetime income during each period of their income producing years. They suggest the long-run consumption function captures this effect. The distribution of these consumption

expenditures is a matter of the individual's tastes and preferences. However, because the distribution of the population by age and income is relatively constant, the individual consumption functions can be aggregated to produce an overall consumption function. The life-cycle hypothesis is based on the model in Boxes 5.3-5.4 (Ruby 2002).

DEFINITION OF MAXIMUM UTILITY DERIVED FROM CONSUMPTION

$\max U_t = \Sigma^L[U(C_t)(1-\delta)^{-t}]$ where (5.3)

$\max U_t$ = maximization of utility from consumption over time
$U(C_t)$ = satisfaction received from consumption in time period t
C_t = level of consumption
δ = the rate of time preference between present and future activity
$(1+r)^{-t}$
W_O = initial level of income producing assets

DEFINITION OF CONSUMPTION DERIVED FROM INCOME AND WEALTH

$\Sigma^L(C_t)(1+r)^{-t} = \Sigma^N Y_t(1+r)^{-t} + W_O$ (5.4)

This theoretical approach is an effort to specify a consumption function based on the lifetime earnings of the *average* individual (emphasis mine). This argument is based on the empirical observations that a random sample of individual/households would reveal disproportionate shares of young or old individuals at the lower end of the income distribution and disproportionate shares of middle age individuals at the upper end of the income distribution.

This theory suggests the young and old households have a high average propensity to consume and may even be engaged in dissavings. The young may borrow against future earnings, while the old may spend-down their life savings. This is compared with middle-aged individuals/households who are either paying off accumulated debt or saving for old age. These conditions affect the average propensities to consume for the three groups. Individual/household income will rise and fall over the business cycle and around these long-run averages of income creating a short-run consumption function.

The permanent-income hypothesis and the life-cycle hypothesis bring to the fore important observations for this chapter. The consumption function is affected by the fact that incomes are distributed at low average levels for younger individuals, at higher average values for those at middle ages, and then at lower average values for older age.

Seater (1998) observes that there have been a number of empirically based rejections of the permanent-income and life-cycle hypothesis models. He suggests that these rejections have occurred because of the characteristics of the aggregate data or from model misspecifications. He suggests that reformulation of the consumption function will provide more accurate results.

This sets the stage for the beginning of the synthesis proposed in this research. This synthesis will be constructed from the disparate background presented in this introduction. Initially, there is the consumption function suggested by Keynes (1936) and reappearing in different forms (for example, Modigliani and Brumberg 1954, Friedman 1957). Central to this research is the determination of how variation in demographic conditions affects or constrains personal consumption. Keynes maintains that levels of consumption depend on "effective demand" which is the consequence of levels of personal income subtracting out taxes and moderated by the individual's/household's marginal propensity to consume and marginal propensity to save. Modigliani and Brumberg (1954) add a more detailed perspective by bringing to the fore the nature of income distributions by *age groupings* (emphasis mine).

Kuznets (1966) adds his perspective to this call for disaggregation as a path to better understanding economic growth. Kuznets (1966) maintains the *different impact of population growth on distinct economic groups within a nation merits further analysis* (emphasis mine). He did not suggest what those units of analysis and the detailed nature of that analysis might be.

An obvious, but necessary fact to this theoretical view is that levels of personal income from all sources both permit and restrict personal consumption. The importance of this condition is made more evident by Creamer's (1956) finding that variation in personal income levels corresponds on a one-to-one basis with the variation of business cycles." This fact makes the examination of conceptual or theoretical variables related to variations in personal income a focus of this research.

Understandings about variations in personal income are enhanced by the understandings initially developed by Schultz (1960, 1963) and later Becker (1975). Their addition of the value of education, experience and training as *human capital* (emphasis mine) to economic growth and well-being contributed to understanding of its role in promoting economic growth. Denison (1962, 1974) empirically assessed the role of the "quality" of labor in economic growth in the United States. His analysis was later used for comparative purposes by Kuznets (1966). Kuznets (1966, 1973) developed estimates of the proportionate role of the human factor and the *quality of labor* (emphasis mine) in modern economic growth within the United States and across a selection of developed nations.

Importantly, there were unexplained residuals in efforts to explain economic growth. Kuznets (1966) found through his empirical deductions that about one-third of the rate of growth was unaccounted for and called this "residual efficiency." While Solow concentrates on the role of labor and capital in the growth of output, there is the Solow residual which appears to account for approximately 50 per cent of the growth in the private economy during the 1874–1950 period (Blanchard and Fischer 1998).

The insights of Keynes in his Galton Lecture to the *Eugenics Society* (1937) offer additional insight for those interested in understanding some aspects of economic asymmetry. In this speech, Keynes notes the expectation of continuing population growth (in the developed world—comment mine) is not a given. He acknowledges that the time lag effects of vital statistics can be observed. Population decline is one such possibility. He states, "An era of increasing population tends to promote optimism." In an era of declining population demand, which tends to be based on current rather than future conditions, a state of over-supply is likely to occur. Demand for capital declines in the situation of a declining population. The demand for capital becomes dependent on the increase in the average level of consumption, the increased demands of a growing population, the demands of new inventions or improvements, or a decline in interest rates. In summarizing, Keynes states "a phase of declining population will make it immensely more difficult than before to maintain prosperity."

A related viewpoint is made more general by Staehle (1937) who suggests that the distribution of incomes from earnings ranks in importance with the amount of incomes from earnings in its usefulness in explaining variations in the ratio of retail sales to labor income.

An added aspect of economic asymmetry has been the study of asymmetries in information. Riley (2001) provides a review of this literature. Of most relevance is the work of Shapiro and Stiglitz (1984) in which they propose an information-based explanation of unemployment. An employee's wage exceeds the wage level that would make him indifferent to staying on a job. Employers observe employees to insure that their work effort is maintained. If they do not maintain a satisfactory level of work effort, the employee is fired and is at risk of having wages lower than his former wage. This optimizing behavior of employer and employee is the source of equilibrium unemployment. This view is said to account for the efforts of employees to maintain employment.

In more recent research on business cycles, Diebold and Rudebusch (1999) maintain that evidence of "duration dependence" of business cycles is important to understanding macroeconomic variations. They restate earlier findings offering six *general* conclusions about the nature and occurrence of expansions and contractions. They search for mathematical techniques and methods for application to prediction of turning points and switching behavior of the business cycle. They document the United States Commerce Department's Composite Coincident Index which closely monitors the business cycle for the 1952.1–1993.1 period. Of interest to this research are the four component indices (personal income minus transfer payments, an index of industrial production, manufacturing and trade sales, and employees on non-agricultural payrolls) suggested to be evident of a common factor underlying economic activity. The presence of common turning points, or switching times for these four quantities are taken by Diebold and Rudebusch (1999) to be suggestive of some underlying model or factor. They question the application of nonlinear models in light of the success of linear models and proceed to suggest and test (with mixed results) some alternative models.

Of importance to this theoretical presentation is what appears to be the primary importance of the four component indices of the United States Commerce Department's Composite Coincident Index. When this is compared to the National Bureau of Economic Research's dating process for business cycles, the similarity of the four measures permits narrowing the focus on what is important to understanding the empirical dynamics of economic fluctuations. The observations and documentation provided by Creamer (1956) suggest that understanding the dynamics of personal income represents a worthwhile focus for the development of an inductively-based theoretical framework. Second, the theoretical underpinning of Keynesian economics suggests the primary role of effective demand or personal consumption. The understanding that personal consumption represents approximately two-thirds of United States economic activity provides further reason for trying to understand both theoretically and empirically the nexus of personal income and personal consumption and their influence on economic variations.

The resolution of how demographic change affects the economic asymmetry is, however, more complex than concentrating on singular aspects of the dynamics in an economic system. Defining the economic changes in non-homogeneous societies due to: changing population numbers; age groups with changing incomes; changing human capital or quality of labor levels; changing consumption functions; and, the changing effects of government taxation requires a theoretical view that permits integration of these and other aspects of individual/household participation in an economy. It is this theoretical and applied task, this research addresses.

THE Q-STATE ALGORITHM

Understanding the relationship of demand and supply at aggregated as well as disaggregated levels is facilitated by two theoretical properties. The first is that of the Q-State algorithm (see Equations 5.5–5.13).

$$S_t = A_t - Q_t$$

where, (5.5)

S_t = the stress level present in the relationship between A_t and Q_t
A_t = the actual value of a quantity or variable
Q_t = the equilibrium value of a quantity or variable

Making this relationship dynamic:

$$\frac{dS}{dt} = \frac{dA}{dt} - \frac{dQ}{dt} \qquad (5.6)$$

At a disaggregated level:

$$\frac{dS_z}{dt} = \frac{dA_z}{dt} - \frac{dQ_z}{dt} \qquad (5.7)$$

where z = a good or service, or a category of goods or services

The actual value (A_{zt}) may be related to the equilibrium (Q_{zt}) by any mathematical function or may be random.

APPLYING THE Q-STATE EQUATION(S)

The next step is to apply the Q-State equation to aggregate demand (AD) and aggregate supply (AS). At equilibrium (see Equations 5.8–5.13).

At equilibrium $AD_t = AS_t$ (5.8)

Substituting in the Q-State algorithm:

$AD_t = Q_t$ and $AS_t = A_t$

$S_t = AS_t - AD_t$ or dynamically, (5.9)

$$\frac{dS}{dt} = \frac{dAS}{dt} - \frac{dAD}{dt} \quad (5.10)$$

At equilibrium, $\frac{dS}{dt} = 0$ (5.11)

Disequilibrium in the primary dynamic equation can occur in two directions with a variety of magnitudes and components. Initially:

If $AD_t > AS_t$ then $S_t < 0$ (5.12)

If $AD_t < AS_t$ then $S_t > 0$ (5.13)

BOX 5.11-5.13

PRICES, OUTPUT, AND DEMAND

To more fully define aggregate demand and aggregate supply it is necessary to decompose each into component parts of demand-quantity (O^D), demand-price (Pr^D), supply-quantity (O^S), and supply-price (Pr^S) (see Boxes 5.14–5.17)

Again, the balance or imbalance of an economy is measured by the magnitude and composition of the stress term (dS/dt). As will later be proven, the stress term can take on a variety of values although always consistent with the terms on the right-hand side of the equation. Similarly, for disaggregated supply:

$$AD_t = (O^D_t)\,(Pr^D_t) \qquad (5.14)$$

$$AS_t = (O^S_t)\,(Pr^S_t) \qquad (5.15)$$

Similar equations are used to represent disaggregated demand and disaggregated supply and their components.

$o^d_{z,t}$ = demand-quantity for goods or services in category z or of kind z at time t

$pr^d_{z,t}$ = demand-price for goods or services in category z or of kind z at time t

Therefore:

$$AD_t = \sum_{z=1}^{z=m} (o^d_{z,t})(pr^d_{z,t}) \qquad (5.16)$$

$o^s_{z,t}$ = the supply-quantity of goods or services in category z or of kind z at time t

$pr^s_{z,t}$ = the supply-price for goods or services in category z or of kind z at time t

Therefore: $$AS_t = \sum_{s=1}^{s=m} (o^s_{z,t})(pr^s_{z,t}) \qquad (5.17)$$

Substituting in equation (5.11):

$$S_t = \sum_{z=1}^{z=n} (o^s_{z,t})(pr^s_{z,t}) - \sum_{z=1}^{z=n} (o^d_{z,t})(pr^d_{z,t}) \qquad (5.18)$$

$$\frac{d\,S}{d\,t} = \frac{d \sum_{z=1}^{z=n} (o^s_z)(pr^s_z) - \sum_{z=1}^{z=n} (o^d_z)(pr^d_z)}{d\,t} \qquad (5.19)$$

AGGREGATE SUPPLY BOX 5.18-5.19

CLASSIFYING ECONOMIC SHOCKS

All economic shocks can be classified by their initial impact on one of the dimensions of equations (5.16) or (5.17). A straightforward way of saying this is that all economic shocks affect demand-quantity, demand-price, supply-quantity, and/or supply-price at some level of disaggregation or aggregation. Table 5.2 presents a general framework for the classification of the initial impacts of economic shocks.

Economic shocks, including those associated with monetary policy or lack thereof, can be classified using this framework.

A point of clarification needs to be addressed. When there is available supply-quantity at a given supply-price $(q^s_{z,t})(pr^s_{z,t})$, and a given demand-quantity at a demand-price $(q^d_{z,t})(pr^d_{z,t})$, a transaction occurs when the

TABLE 5.2: Categories of Economic Shocks

Supply-quantity	Supply-price	Demand-quantity	Demand-price
supply-quantity shortfall	supply-price increase (inflation)	excess demand-quantity	demand-price decrease
supply-quantity-excess	supply-price decrease (deflation)	demand-quantity shortfall	demand-price increase
constant supply-output	constant supply-prices	constant demand-quantity	constant demand-price

supply-price of the supplier agrees with the demand-price of the individual or organization interested in consumption. The price at which the transaction takes place is the transaction-price or purchase price. The units of the transaction are the transaction-quantity. If $(q^s_{z,t})(pr^s_{z,t}) > (q^d_{z,t})(pr^d_{z,t})$, there is over-supply or prices are too high. In such situations transactions will not occur. If $(q^s_{z,t})(pr^s_{z,t}) < (q^d_{z,t})(pr^d_{z,t})$, transactions are highly probable and increased production or increases in prices are likely to occur.

A variety of conditions affect supply-price and demand-price and the ability to make transactions for individuals, business, and government. One of the more significant constraints is the level of personal wealth and disposable personal income of the individual consumer. Increasing or decreasing levels of personal disposable income, depending on saving levels, the marginal propensity to consume, and inflation levels affect the ability of the individual to consume. These considerations also affect demand-quantity. Through their changing effect on demand-quantity and demand-price, they effect changes in supply-quantity and supply-price.

For business, a significant combination of constraints is presented by the costs of production a desired profit margin. To sustain a profit, a business must insure that its markets. To do this the costs of production or the levels of profit must be adjusted. Costs of production are adjusted through changes in productivity. Changes in profit are of concern for two reasons. Increasing unit profits risks giving competitors a supply-price edge. Secondly, decreasing profits can threaten the sustainability of a business and adversely affect those who own it and benefit by its continuation. This will be further addressed.

Government is affected by changes in the four components of aggregate demand (see Box 5.20) this in turn affects taxes. This is, in part, determined by the nature of the taxing structure. Consumption taxes such as the sales tax have a different impact than income taxes. Within income taxes, the type of income tax can also be expected to make a difference in tax receipts. A second effect is the ability of the government to make transactions at desirable demand-quantity and demand-price levels. The government as consumer, for example, of medical care is based on its capacity to strike an agreement on transaction or purchase prices and the demand-quantities for a range of medical goods and services. This, in turn, affects the supply-quantity and supply-price position of business.

PERSONAL CONSUMPTION AND AGGREGATE DEMAND (AD)

Decomposing personal consumption (PC) to the individual level demonstrates one set of constraints on personal consumption (see Box 5.21).

Thus, dynamically aggregated demand for a nation state can be represented as:

$$\frac{d\,AD}{d\,t} = \frac{d\,(PC + GDPI + G + X)}{d\,t} \tag{5.20}$$

PC = aggregate personal consumption
GDPI = aggregate gross domestic private investment
G = government expenditures
X = net exports

$$\frac{d\,PC}{d\,t} = \frac{d \sum_{i=1}^{i=n} (y^p_i - tx^p_i - s^p_i - dp^p_i - in_i) + (ds^p_i) + (g^p_i)_{i=1}}{N d\,t} \tag{5.21}$$

y^p_i = amount of an individual's (i) personal income at time t
tx^p_i = amount of taxes paid by an individual (i) at time t
s^p_i = savings amount for an individual (i) at time t
dp^p_i = amount of debt paid by an individual (i) at time t
in_i = social insurance payments
ds^p_i = amount of accumulated debt spent on goods or services by individual (i) at time t
g^p_i = the amount of money spent out of accumulated wealth and savings by individual (i) at time t

DEFINITION OF PERSONAL CONSUMPTION (PC) BOX 5.21

Exploring the constraints on personal income further, the aggregate amount of personal income will be emphasized. In the equations in Box 5.22 the total value of aggregate personal income (Y^P) is constrained by the terms on the right-hand side of the equation. Likewise, if one took each of the remaining terms on the right-hand side of equations in Box 5.22 and developed similar mathematical expressions (the individual's totals summed; the total number and the mean multiplied; and, the number in each subgroup multiplied by the mean for the subgroup) the role of each of these terms in constraining personal consumption would be further elucidated.

$$Y^P = \sum_{i=1}^{i=n} y^P_I \qquad \text{or, alternatively} \qquad (5.22)$$

$$\overline{Y}^P = N\, y^P_i \qquad \text{where } N = \text{the number of individuals with personal income}$$

$\overline{y}^P_i$ = mean personal income for all individuals with personal income

Third,

$$Y^P = \sum_{z=1}^{z} N_z \overline{y}^P_z \qquad \text{where } N_z = \text{the number of individuals in subgroup with personal income} \qquad (5.23)$$

${}^x y^P_z$ = mean personal income of for all individuals in subgroup z with personal income

Decomposing personal consumption (PC) to the subgroup (z) level demonstrates another view of constraints on personal consumption. These terms have a very important role in characterizing economic growth as well as economic downturns. It is of special note that if the number of individuals with personal income in a subgroup declines while their real personal income remains constant, the total real personal income for the subgroup will decline. Furthermore, if there are significant declines in the numbers of individuals in one or more subgroup, the rate of increase or decline in total real personal income can be affected.

The equations in Box 5.22–5.23 also emphasizes the role of the mean real personal income for each subgroup as a component of total constant dollar personal income. Significant differences in mean personal income between subgroups in a society are a source of variation that causes aggregate real personal income to vary. Depending on the magnitude of the other variables in the equations in Box 5.17 they can also be an important source of variation in personal income and constraint on personal consumption. Remaining is a discussion of the role of participation in the personal income economy and its impact on overall real or nominal personal income.

PARTICIPATION IN THE PERSONAL INCOME ECONOMY

There are numerous ways of participating in the personal income portion of the economy. The individual can participate through employment earnings, adjusted proprietors' income, personal dividend income, personal interest income, transfer payments to individuals, pensions, minus personal contributions for social insurance. Personal income available for spending and savings is termed disposable personal income.

What has been important in the past to defining the amount of personal income has been the need to define a unit of analysis. Efforts to use the household as the unit of analysis are problematic as there may be multiple household members with some source of personal income. Trying to define total personal income for a household unit with multiple members presents significant definitional and data collection issues. Thus, this presentation identifies the subgroup with defined characteristics (z) as the unit of analysis.

Subgroups of individuals with characteristics z may have different rates of participation in the personal income economy. If the entire subpopulation represented by the subgroup z is participating in the personal income economy, their personal income participation rate at time t ($PIPR_{z,t}$) equals one. The range of values for participation in the personal income economy by each subgroup is presented in Box 5.24.

$$0 \leq PIPR_{z,t} \leq 1 \qquad 5.24$$

Thus, it is possible to now examine the composition of the total population of a nation-state to facilitate understanding of how population decomposition can be used to understand variation in total real personal income. This decomposition uses variation in the numbers in population subgroups, subgroup mean real personal income, and subgroup personal income participation rates to develop an understanding of real personal income trends in the economy of the nation-state (see Box 5.25).

DEFINING TOTAL POPULATION BOX 5.25

$$TOTPOP_t = \sum_{z=1}^{z=n} POP_{z,t} \tag{5.25}$$

$TOTPOP_t$ = the total population of individuals of age to be earners or recipients of personal income at time t

$POP_{z,t}$ = the population subgroup (z) with defined ethnic, sex, and age attributes and of age to be earners or recipients of personal income at time t

This brings us to a way of stating a population subgroup relationship that affects the size of $y^P_{z,t}$, and Y^P_t. This relationship is found in Box 5.26.

Thus, the role of population subgroups, their real mean personal income, and their participation in the personal income economy is established. Total real personal income and its components of personal savings and personal spending are moderated by debt payments, debt acquisition and expenditure, and wealth liquidation as a constraint on personal consumption. Since personal consumption plays a proportionately large role in a nation-state economy, the role of these three categories of variables is an important contributing influence to macroeconomic dynamics.

DEFINING PERSONAL INCOME BOX 5.26

$$(POP_{z,t})(PIPR_{z,t}) = P^{L}_{z,t} + P^{L+O}_{z,t} + OTH_{z,t} \qquad (5.26)$$

where: $P^{L}_{z,t}$ = the number of individuals in subgroup z with income from labor only;

$P^{L+O}_{z,t}$ = employed individuals with labor income and other sources of personal income;

$OTH_{z,t}$ = the number of other individuals in subgroup Z with personal income from only sources other than labor and wealth;

and,

$$E^{L}_{z,t} = P^{L}_{z,t} + P^{L+O}_{z,t}$$

$N^{PI}_{z,t}$ = the number in each population subgroup z with personal income

$$Y^{P}_{z,t} = (POP_{z,t})(PIPR_{z,t})(\bar{y}^{P}_{z,t})$$

$$\frac{d\,Y^{P}}{d\,t} = \frac{d \sum_{z=1}^{z=n} (POP_{z,t})(PIR_{z,t})(\bar{y}^{P}_{z,t})}{d\,t}$$

It is important to note that within the economies of different nation states, the characteristics used to identify subgroups with significantly different levels of personal income may differ from these presented here. For example the categories might be age sex, and education level. The categories of ethnicity, sex, and age are used here because they offer a method of distinguishing how the labor market of one economy values human and social capital.

EVIDENCE FROM VARIATIONS OF ONE ETHNIC SUBGROUP

The theory advanced in this research is supported by evidence prepared from estimates and projections prepared by the United States Census Bureau (2002) and data from March Current Population Survey (2002). The U.S. Census Bureau prepares population estimates and projections. The March Current Population Survey is conducted by the U.S. Census Bureau for the U.S. Department of Labor and provides annual estimates of personal income for ethnic and age subgroups within the United States population. An important caveat in the interpretation of these data is there is an undetermined amount of underreporting of income on the March Current Population Survey.

Three figures for the White, Non-Hispanic Male subgroup will be presented. These figures are in keeping with the theoretical framework presented as they show the number of White, Non-Hispanic Males by age subgroup (Figure 5.1), the mean personal income by subgroup (Figure 5.2), and the total real personal income (in 2000 constant dollars) by age subgroup (Figure 5.3).

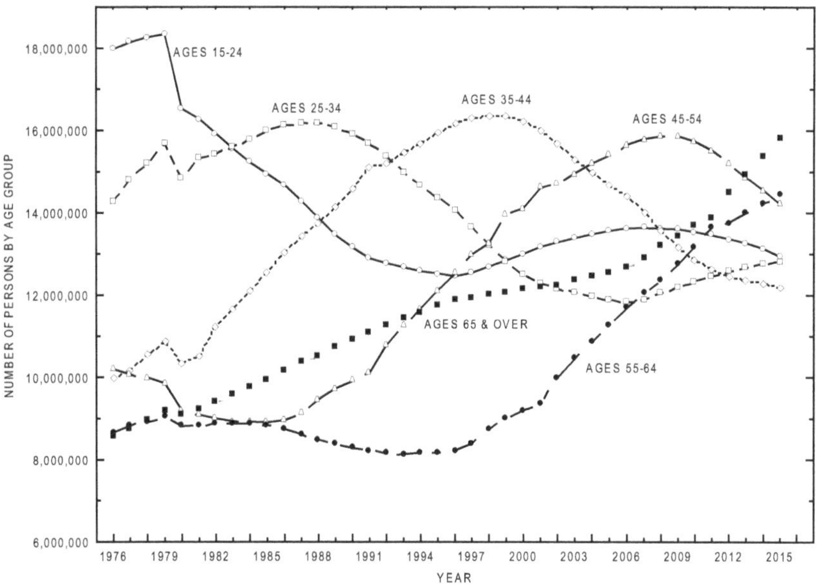

FIGURE 5.1: Number of White, Non-Hispanic Males in the U.S. by Age Subgroup

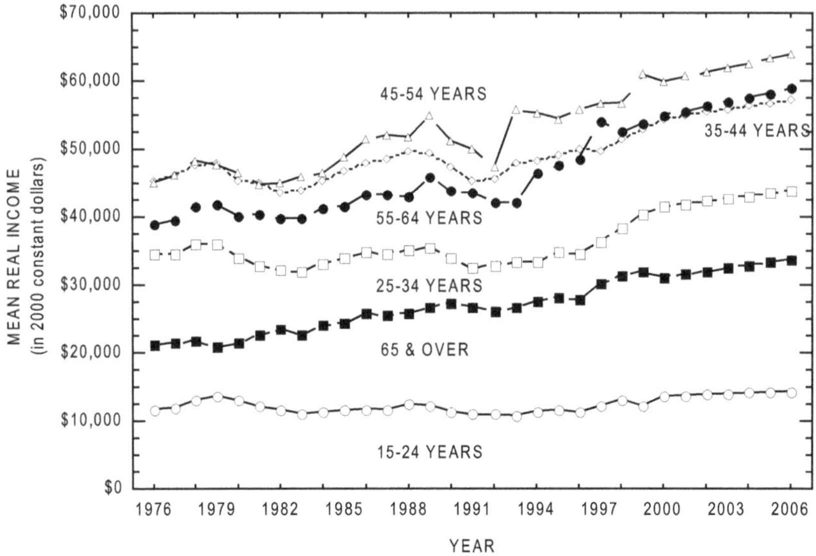

Source: U.S. Bureau of Census, March Current Population Survey, 2001-2006 projections

FIGURE 5.2: Mean Real Income for White, Non-Hispanic Males, 1976-2006

All figures for the 1976 – 2000 period are based on March Current Population Survey values. From 2000–2006 are estimations based on an inflation rate of 1.6 percent for personal income, and no fiscal stimulus. The personal income participation rate assumed after 2000 was the mean personal income participation rate for each subgroup from 1980–2000.

Figure 5.1 shows the complex variation of the numbers of individuals in each of the six identified age subgroups. This variation can be traced back to annual variations in the number of live births for each year of age, patterns of cohort survival, and the variation in the net immigration for individuals into or out of each individual year of age and their survival patterns. In Figure 5.1 these effects are summarized in the number of surviving individuals in each ten-year age subgroup. Of particular note are the declining numbers of individuals in the 25–34 year old subgroup and the 35–44 year old subgroup.

These declines will be reflected in declines in total personal income for these age subgroups in Figure 5.3.

Figure 5.2 details the changing real mean personal income levels of each age subgroup of White, Non-Hispanic males. Real mean personal income tends to be a relatively "sticky" variable within a given age subgroup. Because of the differences in mean values between age subgroups at any given time,

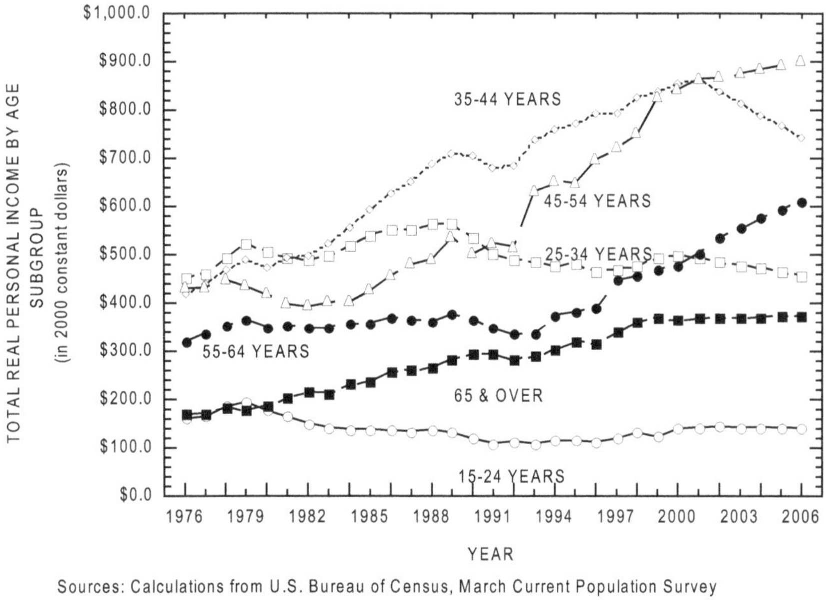

FIGURE 5.3: Total Real Personal Income for White, Non-Hispanic Males, 1976-2006

this figure makes apparent that mean incomes are also a significant source of variation in total real personal income across the age subgroups.

Figure 5.3 was prepared by multiplying population subgroup size, the personal income participation rate, and mean real personal income for each White, Non-Hispanic male subgroup for a given year. As such it represents the total real personal income attributable to the subgroup for each year from 1976–2006. The values for 2001–2006 are projected based on a 1.6 percent rate of inflation and no major government fiscal stimulus.

The last step is the aggregation of the subtotals for the six age subgroups into a total real personal income estimate for all White, Non-Hispanic males by year from 1976–2006. Figure 5.4 contains the result of that summation. The summation of this complex of subgroup real total personal income values yields results that are not well understood from examining the individual real income patterns from Figure 5.3. What is presented is a period of slowly declining total real personal income for White, Non-Hispanic males in the 2000–2006 period. This has implications for the levels of consumption to be expected that are independent of debt accumulation and the use of stocks of savings and wealth.

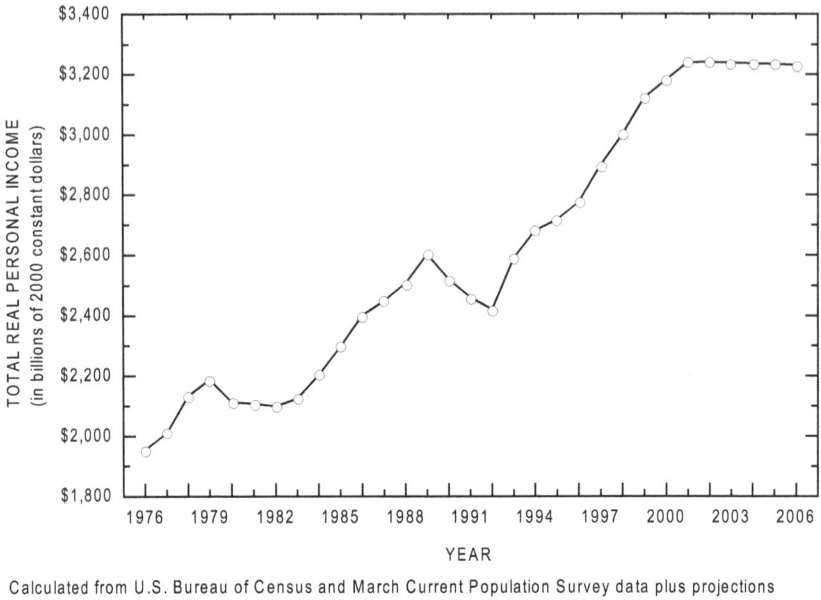

FIGURE 5.4: Total Real Income for White, Non-Hispanic Males, 1976-2006

DISCUSSION AND CONCLUSIONS

The initial sections presenting algorithms for aggregated and disaggregated demand and supply are presented to emphasize the truism that disequilibria can come from a variety of sources. It is of some importance that incidents and periods known as price shocks have an impact on demand-quantity and demand-price. In the end, as seen from Figure 4 such periods get reflected in periods of declining personal income. It is important to determine the extent to which the price shocks are responsible for such declines and the extent to which demographic change precedes or is coincident with such changes. For example, is an increase in oil prices due to a declining of the consuming population (i.e. does a decline in consumption due to decline in population subgroup numbers precede the price increases)? And does this increase in prices further accent a period of decline?

Furthermore, one can come to understand growth as a dynamic of disequilibrium, generally in the direction of demand-quantity and demand price exceeding the supply side dualism of supply-quantity and supply-price. The alternative of misreading the level of demand-quantity, demand-price by business can lead to conditions of over-supply related to either supply-quantity or supply-cost.

The equations to which the Q-State algorithm is applied permit the stress term or side of the equation to assume a variety of values that are essential to keep the equation in balance, while at the same time representing economic balance, equilibrium, imbalance, or disequilibrium. Since these are valid equations, manipulation of the terms of the equations permits the exploration of a number of business dynamics or dynamics related to personal income and population variation.

The research presents a way of conceptualizing the influence of demographic variables on personal income in an economy. The conceptualization relies on the ability of the economist and demographer to distinguish distinct subgroups of individuals whose real or nominal personal income is significantly different than that of other defined subgroups. The term individual is emphasized because of the complex array of household units that exist. In a household there may be multiple earners and persons receiving other forms of personal income. To establish mutual exclusivity, the terms of the analysis and projections must be at the individual level.

The identification of the number of individuals in a particular demographic classification for which information on nominal or real personal income is available is a necessary and sufficient basis for the development of an applied data series. This will permit the application of the algorithms set forth in equations in boxes 5.22 and 5.23 of this research.

A further implication of this research is, if the number of live births and the attendant sex-ratios are available for a given subgroup, the number of survivors at each age may be relatively accurately estimated. This assumes the availability of accurate life tables (Whelpton 1928, Shryock and Siegel 1973). Secondly, accurate net immigration data by subgroup is needed to supplement the live birth and life table data. These data form a foundation for estimating population into the future. This permits approximately a ten to twelve year advance perspective on population changes in the absence of special circumstances or changes such as war.

Last, it is hypothesized that similar demographic trends have been partially, if not primarily responsible for economic malaise in nations such as Japan, Germany, and England. Further research needs to be conducted in these and other nations to determine if applying algorithms similar to those developed in this chapter explains their changing levels of personal income as well as the related dynamics of personal consumption.

CHAPTER 6

The United States Innovation Revolving Fund (USIRF)

INTRODUCTION

This document sets forth the general outline of a plan for a federally funded (by loans) and independently operated research and development revolving fund. To become reality the concept needs to be translated into law and funded at a sufficiently high level to have an impact on United States (U.S.) universities, businesses, individuals, and employment. The proposal takes advantage of the tasks which Americans and American individuals, universities, businesses do best: innovate and spread innovations.

GENERAL DESIGN

The following is the general design of the proposal followed by specific enabling conditions and prohibitions. The United States House of Representatives, Senate, and the President shall enact into law a bill termed the UNITED STATES INNOVATION REVOLVING FUND ACT. The legislation shall include the following elements:

- A management group shall be appointed of scientists and innovative businessmen (the Board of Directors) to advise an agency titled the U.S. INNOVATION REVOLVING FUND. This agency shall be directly responsible to the U.S. Department of Energy. Other lines of responsibility are to the Secretary of the Department of Energy, USIRF Board of Directors, the President, and to the Congress of the United States.

- This agency shall be funded adequately to insure that each project is reviewed biannually and is making substantive progress. Accompanying these reviews will be annual review of the projects' fiscal health. The budget of the agency shall be proposed and acted upon by the Executive, the House of Representatives, and the Senate.
- The Agency shall have the power to terminate a business's participation or levy fines for cost overruns, fiscal mismanagement, or accounting irregularities.
- Businesses, universities, and individuals receiving funding for specified projects shall use government funding only for the purpose(s) specified.
- A select group of scientists, engineers, and innovators (7 in number) and innovative businessmen (4 in number) shall serve as a Board of Directors to which the management group must report on a quarterly basis. This reporting shall include interim monthly reports by the management group.
- The members of the Board of Directors shall receive compensation for their period of service on the Board.
- The CEO of the USIRF will be both the CEO and the Chairperson of the Board of Directors at the same time. His/her term of service may be two consecutive terms of six years each interrupted by six years followed again by one or two six-year terms.
- The individuals who serve on the Board of Directors shall serve terms of 6 years. A member of the Board of Directors may serve two consecutive terms.
- The management group shall develop areas of research and/or development in which project proposals are to be solicited from individuals, educational institutions, and businesses. Persons having no college aspirations may also apply for project funding.
- The Board of Directors shall suggest and discuss projects. The appropriate agency will develop, renew, and recommend projects for the choice of the Board of Directors. The Board of Directors shall have access to all proposals.
- Proposals shall be submitted by individuals, universities, and businesses to the management group. The proposals shall conform to the guidelines issued in the USIRF call for proposals. After review and scoring, the proposals shall be submitted to the Board of Directors for decision on which proposals to fund. This will be an expedited process.
- Examples of the type of research and development projects include, but are not limited to: improving the mileage and sale of efficient automobiles; construction of bike trails along roadsides, bike paths, and connecting routes; the development and improvement of all types of communication; airplane structural and engine technology; the development and sale of

usable hydrogen and oxygen engines and turbines; the process of making cold fusion feasible; agricultural development of more efficient bio-fuels and their production; light rail projects; high speed rail projects between major cities of the U.S.; efficient aircraft; nanotechnology; computer technology; development of new materials, the development and production of new methods of manufacturing; improvement of waste management for all types of materials; improving the efficiency of all types of energy and electricity production with an emphasis on those means of energy production that are renewable. This would include geothermal, solar, water, wind, and quantum electric energy production.

- Scholarships shall be funded and granted to individuals entering the fields of engineering, product development, and product research at both the undergraduate and graduate levels.
- The funding shall include efforts and materials necessary for the research of the targeted innovation or improvement. Funding proposals may include funds for the preparation of prototypes, manufacture for consumption, marketing, and sale of the innovation or improvement.
- The marketing of innovations or improvements may include existing products that promote the goals of energy efficiency and pollution control and elimination.
- The grantee shall repay the USIRF grants at an annual rate established by the USIRF. No interest shall be charged. One hundred percent of the USIRF's grants shall be repaid.
- The USIRF shall establish a revolving fund to pay out grant monies and receive repayments from grantees. The revolving fund shall be funded annually by federal appropriations. The funding level shall be adequate to meet existing demand.
- All copyrights and patents resulting from the research and development activity from USIRF grants shall be the property of the United States government and shall not be sold. A percentage of net profits accruing to the USIRF as a result of copyrights and patents shall be deposited in the revolving fund. As an incentive, profits from the development of copyrights and patents will be awarded to the developer of the copyrights and patents at a rate of 15 percent for the developer, 70 percent for the university or business organization producing the product, and 15 percent for the USIRF.
- The developing individual, university, or business shall have exclusive rights to the manufacture, marketing, and sale of products they develop for a period of ten years from the termination of the grant(s).
- Funds from the USIRF may be used to expand the use of existing innovations and improvements.

- Each separate project granted by the USIRF shall have a chart of accounts separate from all other accounts maintained by the individual, organization, or business.
- Grantees of the grants awarded by the USIRF shall be U.S. based citizens, residents, universities, and businesses that pay taxes in the U.S. and have offices and plants in the U.S. All projects will be located in the U.S.
- The developed products shall be produced exclusively in the U.S.
- All projects requiring from $1 to $50,000,000 per annum in government funds shall meet three conditions. The originator(s) of the project will have (1) met with at least 5 persons who would use the project, (2) the technology or device will pay for itself within 3–5 years, and (3) the innovation or improvement will be used by 250,000 or more individuals or 10 businesses or universities. This approach is modeled after a similar program developed by International Development Enterprises. The project shall be subject to the same payback and profit sharing conditions as projects requiring more funding.

JUSTIFICATION FOR GOVERNMENT SUPPORT

The grants proposed herein support research and development that will have effects for generations. The grants will enable the completion of research, development, and production of products for which individuals and businesses can see no immediate return but for which a demand is present. Because of the unique qualities of research and development in some of the mentioned areas, an individual, university, or business may experience obstacles to securing loans and other forms of capital.

This proposal recommends putting in place a law and an appropriation that will ensure the lead of the U.S. in the development of new ideas and products. While doing this, the proposed law will invest in four types of capital: innovation capital; business capital; human capital; and, social capital. New jobs will be developed that will range across the range of incomes from executives, managers, supervisors, production workers, engineers, scientists, chemists, teachers, etc.

In summary, this proposal represents a method of injecting funds into the U.S. economy that will have a multiplier effect. It challenges individuals, universities, and businesses to innovate and merchandise products in the spirit of American entrepreneurship. It joins the federal government in a partnership with the creative forces of American life to encourage their development and growth.

CHAPTER 7

Why Business Cycles?

The thesis of this paper is that variation in live births and the demographic characteristics of sex, ethnicity, age, and subgroup mean income are responsible for economic expansions and contractions. Data from the Current Population Survey (CPS) Annual Social and Economic Supplement (ASEC) are used to categorize the number of individuals in each general category. Mean personal income for each group is multiplied by the number of income receivers in the group to calculate total personal income per group. Personal consumption is derived from personal income, taxes, savings, and debt. The results for each group are summed to calculate total personal income for all those receiving income. Validation of the comparability of estimated personal income to actual personal income is made.

BACKGROUND

Alternative Theories of Business Cycles

Economic expansion is a period of increasing economic activity. Economic contraction is a period of declining economic activity. In the United States (U.S.) the National Bureau of Economic Research's Business Cycle Dating Committee officially determines a downturn's beginning and end. The Dating committee determines the peaks and troughs of business cycles (in terms of quarters). The fact these decisions are made quarterly creates some dissonance with annual data.

The central purpose of this research article is to propose mathematical relationships, based in demographic and economic changes that explain most occurrences of economic asymmetry. There are generally two approaches to developing theories for testing hypotheses: the deductive and the inductive approaches. The deductive approach involves developing a theory and applying that theory to a specific case. The alternative, used in this research, is an inductive approach in which observations of data lead to the development of theory. The study of economic asymmetry has been a field in which both methods of theoretical development have been employed.

The theory of economic asymmetry has a long history of both intellectual and practical concern. Stannett (2002) has identified five categories of theories of economic asymmetry and business cycle theory developed in the twentieth century: external shocks; inflation; over-production and under-consumption; inappropriate production; and, the nature of capitalism.

Stannett (2002) has reviewed other early 20th century theories of economic asymmetry in which there was movement toward explaining the business cycle itself. May (1902) advanced a theory that production growth necessitated rising wages with falling prices. However, prices ultimately rise and result in over-production. Prices respond by declining until the markets are cleared. Stannett has described Beveridge's 1912 findings that suggest business cycles are a consequence of industrial competition. In a competitive economy, competing producers seek to fulfill potential demand. All the goods produced cannot be sold at a profit. Consequently, there is over-production. Prices fall and adjustment occurs until demand once again exceeds supply and the business cycle is renewed.

Stannett (2002) has reviewed the 1909 work of Hobson who maintains that differences between production and consumption are related to the savings ratio and the fact that a considerable proportion of wealth is concentrated in the hands of a few. During prosperous times the incomes of the wealthy grow rapidly which allows for more savings. The savings are invested in production until a surplus of production occurs, which is accompanied by a drop in prices and a reduction in the incomes of the wealthy. An adjustment in savings occurs until there is balanced consumption. Similar research in 1908 by Bouniatian suggested that if prices rise, those who own goods being marketed experienced a concentration of purchasing power and capital ownership. Accumulation of ownership results in increased investment in production and the means of production. Thus, the growth of productive capacity exceeds the capacity to consume. Prices fall, the demand for investment falls, and the rates of interest on loans for production fall. The cycle is now ready to resume.

Stannett has also written about the 1909 work of Aftalion who proposed that the nature of the production process and related marginal utilities of goods to the consumer were responsible for the presence of business cycles.

If there is unsatisfied demand for goods or services, then producers respond by producing the necessary goods and services. When productive capacity is developing marginal utility of the available goods is high. As production increases, new production results in a reduction of the marginal utility of the goods and services. Production continues and over-production follows. Producers react by restricting investment in production. Eventually, excess demand reoccurs and the marginal utilities of goods and services will rise. The business cycle starts anew.

Stannett (2002) has reported that Spiethoff, in work starting in 1902, explained business cycles in terms of an imbalance between the production of industrial equipment used in production and the production of goods for consumption. Spiethoff hypothesized that the demand for productive capacity can be satisfied in a few years after an imbalance develops. After the demands for productive capacity are met, there is unemployment, reduced consumption, and losses among capitalists. Prices decline, new weak or inefficient producers are forced out, new needs develop, and another cycle resumes.

Lescure's 1907 work referenced by Stannett (2002) suggested that as production increases to satisfy consumer demand, profits decline to the extent that new investment capital is not forthcoming to develop enterprises for continued expansion. This inability to expand constrains the demand for producer goods and depression follows. These conditions result in fewer costly raw materials, lower loan costs, and reduced wages and thus reducing the costs of production.

Fisher, in *The Purchasing Power of Money* (1911), has observed that interest rates have a tendency to rise after increases in inflation. People with greatest foresight seize the opportunity to invest during these periods. Increases in bank borrowing combine with increased velocity of money circulation and prices also tend to increase. The process is self-reinforcing. After a time, interest rates catch up with inflation and the demand for loans declines. Businesses suffer when expansion plans are based on assumptions that interest terms would remain at their original levels. The number and amount of loans start to contract and businesses fail. Money circulation slows and prices fall as the interest rate decline again lags behind. Profits suffer, until interest rates are in balance. This cycle then renews itself.

Mitchell (1913, 1951, and 1961) established many of the issues that are central to the discussion of business cycles and economic asymmetry today. One of those forces that Mitchell introduced is that of economic shocks. The theory of shocks, which has a prominent place in the explanation of specific periods of variation in the economy, is a theoretical framework that admits to the occurrence of special circumstances as a source of economic variation. Thus, dramatic price changes in supplies such as oil, war, major weather or other natural events influencing crop production, high levels of bankruptcy, bank insolvency, and rapid dislocations or advances created by changing technology are examples of shocks. What is of importance about the asymmetries introduced by shocks is that each shock has its own special cause. The lack of a general cause makes the establishment of general theory for this type of economic asymmetry difficult.

Mitchell (1913, 1951, and 1961) was an indefatigable chronicler of movement in the cycles of a myriad of indicators of business, labor, financial, imports, exports, prices, and other statistics. He did all of this in search of a general understanding of the reasons for business cycles. In monitoring the expansion, peak, contraction, and trough phases of thirty-four business cycle series he was able to develop observations related to the segments of business cycles. Mitchell (1951) suggested there are, in every segment of the economy, changes in average reference-cycle standings show greater concentration of movements in an upward (expansion) or downward (contraction) direction than do the observations of individual cycles. Furthermore, he suggested that the variation tends to be greater at the beginning of periods of decline and at the beginnings of periods of expansion. In his 1961 research, Mitchell observed that the transformation of business cycle data has a long practice. He suggested that the search for explanation of business cycle is most likely to be successful if guided by rational hypotheses. These efforts to identify rational hypotheses resulted in the collection of a great deal of data, but also resulted in non-homogenous variations in many of the data series collected.

To summarize, Mitchell (1951), suggested that the net result of random forces acting in any given part of a business cycle may be weak or strong depending on the related cyclical influences. Because these influences remain unidentified, Mitchell, with his customary empirical rigor, suggests, "Even now what we can say is ill proportioned, tentative, and subject to change as investigation proceeds" (p.5, 1951).

Inflation is another source of economic asymmetry. There are two sources of what is perceived as inflation or deflation. Variation in the price of commodities can occur in either direction. Deflation in the United States occurred during the Great Depression years (Friedman and Schwartz, 1963). Inflation was a serious issue in the latter years of the Carter administration (1979–1982) and threatened to disrupt the United States economy. The savings and loan crisis occurred primarily because of the rapid inflation of the 1970s. Interest rates to depositors rose significantly while loans held by institutions were primarily fixed-rate mortgages. The market value of mortgages held by thrift institutions fell so they were worth less than the value of thrift deposits and other obligations.

This common perception of inflation is that which has been identified by Irving Fischer (1928) in his discussion of the "money illusion." He shows that perceptions of the high cost of living due to a rise in the price of commodities can be a result of variation in the monetary unit itself. Money is pegged to a certain value or allowed to float in value with the anticipation of creating a basis for stable currency value. This source of economic asymmetry has repeated itself with serious consequences for the economies involved.

What cannot be doubted is the important role that money has played in economic crises both in the United States and internationally. Periods of hyperinflation in Austria (1919–1922), Hungary (1942–1946), Germany (1917–1923, 1932–1944), Greece (1938–1944), Poland (1921–1924), and Russia (1922–1924) documented by Cagan (1956); and Germany (1938–1944) (Klein 1956) are examples of what happens when the money supply is excessive. Friedman and Schwartz (1963) in their survey of the history of money in the United States make a case for the primacy of money in business cycles and economic change. Their review of the Depression highlights issues that they consider central to the maintenance of economic stability. They perceive that positive growth in the economy is maintained by a modest, but regular growth in the money supply; yet, the money supply equation presented by Friedman (1956) contains a term (u) that stands for unexplained tastes and preferences.

Additional, related theories of economic shock and asymmetry encompass over-production and under-consumption. These related economic concepts are important to understanding economic asymmetries and are at the basis of aggregate supply and demand relationships. These possibilities are partially addressed in a part of the theoretical work presented herein. Whenever issues of over-production and under-consumption are discussed, the issues of supply-price supply-quantity, demand-price, and demand-quantity must be discussed concurrently.

The presence of excess inventories in an economy or in one of its sectors may indicate the presence of over-production or imperfect information. Alternatively, the availability of excess inventories may be a consequence of under-consumption. In the classical view, production of goods is its own source of consumption as production creates the wealth for consumption. Now it is well understood that there are income distribution issues involved in the production of goods and services that cause unevenness in consumption between individuals. The presence of malnutrition is an example of the presence of under-consumption in this revised view of the nature of under-consumption. Asymmetries in production and consumption exist at international, national, and sub-national levels.

When investment is made in the production of goods for which no market can be found there are economic asymmetries. These asymmetries occur for specific businesses or within specific sectors of the economy. Recently, the dot-com boom in the United States economy offers examples of overproduction. In this case innovation created entirely new generations of products.

Structural factors in national economies and the international economic framework may create sources of asymmetry. Private, national, and international economic arrangements may create significant barriers to coordinating levels of supply and demand. The multiplicity of national and private economic actors makes economic imbalance and asymmetries at disaggregated and aggregated levels inevitable.

Easterlin (1965) has summarized findings on the nature of long swings or Kuznets cycles of population and labor force growth in the United States. Cross-sectional data series were used; some were from pre-World War I era, and some extended to 1950. Many series were from decennial population censuses from 1870 to 1950. Early in this period (up until 1920), swings were largely related to immigration. Until 1950 fertility assumed a more important role. The white native-born population showed conformity to long swings throughout the entire period. After 1920, the African-American component also showed conformity to long swings in the labor force. Long swings in output growth typically appear to precede those in the rate of immigration. Evidence points to United States demand conditions as the *systematic* factor resulting in migration swings, which leads to the tentative conclusion that immigration appears to be a result of swings in the rate of economic growth, although such movement may well have played an important functional role.

In summary, up to 1914, long swings in the population and labor force that lasted fifteen to twenty-five years were observed (Easterlin 1965). A speculative interpretation of the swings was presented. A sequence of prior swings in the rate of economic growth, and a rise in aggregate demand associated with business investment were accompanied by a growth of wage rates and a decline in unemployment. Migration from farm areas and abroad to urban centers resulted. During contractions, the same sequence tended to prevail in reverse. From 1914 to 1950, long swings in labor force and population growth continued, but have demonstrated different characteristics. The birth rate assumes a much greater role in the swings. Easterlin (1965) has raised significant questions about the interpretation of these long swings and has noted the need to develop a meaningful analytical model that is consistent with these observations.

To give some idea of the empirical associations between United States population, a series of macro-economic correlations were prepared. The results are found in Table 7.1:

TABLE 7.1: Correlation Matrix of Annual Macroeconomic Indicators 1929–2000 (N=72)*

Variable	PC	AD	UNEMPR	GDPI	GOV	GDP	POP	DPI	M_2
AD	.998	.--							
UN EMPR	-.171**	-.182**	--						
GDPI	.947	..962	-.211**	--					
GOV	.994	.995	-.183**	.942	--				
GDP	.999	.998	- 175**	.948	.996	--			
POP	.885	.973	.961	.779	.936	.894	--		
DPI	-.171**	.999	-.170**	.946	.997	.892	.902	--	
M_2	.992	-.330	-.179**	.940	.997	.992	.909	.993	--
PI	.999	.998	-.174**	.999	.996	.999	.973	.999	.992

*Source: U.S. Department of Commerce, Bureau of Economic Analysis, National Income and Product Accounts; in 1996 constant dollars; Population: U.S. Census Bureau. **p>.05, all others p<.006

DEFINITIONS OF VARIABLES IN TABLE 7.1

POP—United States population
PI—personal income
GDP—Gross domestic product
PC—personal consumption
AD—aggregate demand
UNEMPR—Unemployment rate
PI—personal incomePS—personal savings
GOV—government capital
DPI—disposable personal income expenditures
GDPI—gross domestic private investment M_2—money supply

The study of growth developed by Solow (1970, 1988) is important because it explains the combined influence of the dependence of growth rates of output on labor and capital. The rate of growth of output is stated as:

SOLOW OUTPUT EQUATION AND TERMS

$$g_y = ag_n + (1\text{-}a)g_k + q \qquad (7.1)$$

g_y =output
a = share of labor in output
g_n = growth rate of labor
g_k = growth rate of capital
q = that part of growth that is unexplained by the other variables

Reformulating this equation suggests that the interaction of labor and the other terms in the equation play an important role in economic growth. This term is called multifactor productivity growth, or the Solow residual (see Box 7.2).

$$(g_y - g_n) = \frac{1\text{-}a}{a}\,(g_{nk} - g_y) + \frac{1}{a} \qquad (7.2)$$

The rate of growth of output per man-hour is related positively to the rate of growth of the capital-output ratio and the multifactor productivity growth term. From 1874 to 1986, the output-capital ratio has been relatively constant. Thus, the Solow residual was approximately equal to the share of labor multiplied by the growth rate of labor productivity. During the 1874–1986 period, multifactor productivity (the Solow residual) accounts for over half of the growth in the private economy. However, there is only limited understanding of the source(s) of this residual. Also, explanations of how the stochastic variations characterized by changing unemployment and periods of expansion and decline in output remain inadequate.

Simon Kuznets (1966, 1973) has suggested the increased role of population in economic growth by analyzing the historical role of population increase and growth in per capita production as mutually occurring events in developed economies (1966, pp. 20). Using data from 12 developed nations from 1954 to 1960, Kuznets found that personal income was 88 percent of gross national product. He has also suggested that as economic growth occurs, the share of personal income in total output may change. Kuznets has compared data on the share of labor in national income between 1909–1913 and 1954–1958. He has observed, "The price per man-hour relative to the price per service unit of capital had to rise by the difference between 2.84 and .87 percent per year." This is a price differential of 2.41 between the two periods. Denison (1962, 1974) has provided evidence explaining that the price per man-hour of labor has increased at a faster rate than the price per unit of capital services. He has linked this phenomenon to improvements in the "quality of labor." He suggested that improvements in educational levels account for approximately 0.78 percent per year compared to a growth in total man-hours of labor of 0.87 percent per year. Other sources of change were growth in the efficiency of labor (associated with a reduction in working hours) by 0.43 percent per year and increased efficiency of female labor (0.14 percent). These changes have resulted in an increase in the growth of labor input (in terms of man-hours) from 0.87 to 2.22 percent per year.

National income is divided between labor and capital. Kuznets (1966) has emphasized that "*live* labor" brought about improvements in the proportion of labor as a part of national income. His estimates and those based on Denison's work (1962) suggest that the labor share of national income in the United States was 76.9 percent compared to an actual measured share of 77.3 percent. Thus, the share of labor as a portion of net output had increased in recent decades because of the increased investment in maintaining and improving the quality of labor. Denison's (1962) work emphasized estimating the influence of several factors such as education of the work force, length of workday, spread of knowledge, economies of scale, and sex of worker to understand the growth of product attributable to each factor.

A second approach enlarges the scope of the term capital beyond material stocks to include investment in the education of human beings through formal means or by on-the-job training and experience. This approach was developed by Schultz (1960) and Becker (1975). How does the quality of labor and its educational level factor into understanding economic asymmetry, if it does at all?

Kuznets has suggested there is a residual (*unexplained*) efficiency of growth in output per unit of total input that amounts to approximately one-third of the rate of growth in total input for the 1909 to 1957. These gains in "residual efficiency" are components of the increase in total output that are *not* accounted for by sources of measured inputs. This begs the question "Why this large component of national income due to "residual efficiency?" Is this residual efficiency in any way related to issues of economic asymmetry?

Kuznets (1966) has noted the trends in the distribution in the labor force in six nations over differing periods of time. These trends indicate significant increases in the proportions of individuals with employee status compared to entrepreneurs and the self-employed. Additional changes in occupational status have been accompanied by changes in the distribution of the sex of employees. In Table 4.4 (p. 192) Kuznets presents these changing distributions over the period from 1900 to 1960. Can these demographic factors or others be related to issues of economic asymmetry?

Kuznets (1973) has analyzed the relationship between population growth and *per capita* income for 21 developed nations from the early 1950s to 1964 and finds a negative Spearman correlation ($r = -.434$). However, when four countries that had populations with higher growth rates than those of Europe and Japan were removed, the Spearman correlation became $r = .061$. Kuznets' quantitative efforts are limited, however, by the lack of data necessary to cover important structural divisions in the economy. He suggests (1973):

> Both the effects of population increase on aspects of economic growth other than aggregate income per capita and the differential impact of population growth on distinct economic groups within a country obviously merit further analysis. (p. 48)

This statement is followed by an observation very relevant to this research: the changing levels of population growth and decline alter the number of consumer equivalent units. (pp. 14–15). Kuznets (1973) follows this by stating "material capital stock effectively increases output *only* if it is supplemented by some uses of product now classified as *consumption*" (p. 25) (emphasis mine). This raises another question. How does consumption factor into the occurrence of periods of economic asymmetry?

RELEVANCE OF PERSONAL INCOME: THEORETICAL PERSPECTIVES

The next step in understanding the nature of economic asymmetry is aided by finding an aggregate economic measure that varies directly or similarly, as do business cycles. Business cycles are the economic manifestation of economic asymmetry. As such, having a measure that varies in parallel offers a possible approach to modeling or explaining economic asymmetry. Daniel Creamer's (1956) study of personal income during business cycles provides a longitudinal time series for personal income in the United States that is compared to the peaks and troughs of business cycles over the 1909–1951 periods. To summarize, Creamer (1956) maintains that despite long-term shifts in proprietary, labor, and property income, "there is a one-to-one correspondence of personal income cycles and business cycles." He observes that the turning points in personal income may be measured in current or constant prices with the exception of period of war, its aftermath or periods of rapidly changing prices.

The use of personal income as an explanatory variable for periods of economic asymmetry is reinforced by the existing practices of the National Bureau of Economic Research. The National Bureau of Economic Research (NBER) uses four primary indicators of economic activity to delineate the peaks, duration, and troughs of business cycles (National Bureau of Economic Research, 2002). Economy wide employment, industrial production, real personal income (minus transfer payments) and wholesale-retail sales are the most important NBER indicators when estimating business cycles. A recession begins just after the economy reaches a peak of activity and ends as the economy reaches its trough. Between the trough and the peak the economy is expanding. A recession is defined as "a significant decline in activity across the economy, lasting more than a few months, visible in industrial production, employment, real personal income (minus transfer payments), and wholesale-retail sales." The value of these indicators to the later theoretical developments will become clear.

Different theorists perceive the constraints on personal income in different ways. Keynes (1936) set forth a relatively stable relationship between income, consumption, and savings. He saw consumers as having relatively strong habits and as such changes in the propensity to consume were likely to adjust slowly. Keynes believed that short-term changes in consumption depended primarily on short-term changes in wage-units. Keynes added that as a general rule as income increased, the proportion of income saved increases. The Keynesian consumption function makes it possible to characterize the relationship between disposable income and consumption expenditures.

Keynesian theory (1936) concerned itself with the ability of a market system to maintain full employment and its related stability. The ability of an economy to maintain effective demand was important to his formulation. The level of effective demand is determined in the context of population constraints and the level of technological advancement.

Whereas monetarists and quantity-of-money theorists are concerned with the money supply and its impact on prices, Keynes was interested in the conditions that affect output levels. He was concerned about the conditions that determined the level of employment in an economy. Keynes maintained that the level of employment determined the level of "effective" (or aggregate) demand. In these terms, the Keynesian perspective would maintain there is a steady relationship between aggregate consumption expenditures and aggregate income. This relationship is known as the Absolute Income Hypothesis. Therefore, Keynes argued that decreases or cuts in wages result in declining demand, thereby increasing unemployment.

A general statement of a Keynesian consumption function follows (see Box 7.3) (Ruby 2002).

CONSUMPTION FUNCTION

$$C = ((Y_d)(b)) \pm a \tag{7.3}$$

DEFINITION OF TERMS IN CONSUMPTION FUNCTION

(7.4)

C = consumption expenditures
$\pm a$ = net savings(+) or dissavings (-)
b = the marginal propensity to consume
Y_d = current disposable income

In the Keynesian view, consumption adjusts to the level of income. The level of employment determines the level of income. Levels of investment determine the level of employment. Keynes argued that the level of aggregate demand depends on the level of investment in the economy. If there is no method to determine the correct level of investment in an economy and adjust to that level, full employment will not be achieved.

From the Keynesian perspective, Say's Law (supply creates its own demand) is inoperative. Prices are such that the value of the commodities produced is equal to the value of commodities as a whole. The level of employment at a given wage rate and output at those rates (controlling for population) depends on the marginal propensity to consume and save, the marginal efficiency of capital, the quantity of money, and liquidity preference. Effective demand (or aggregate demand) operates through the propensity to consume, the propensity to save, new investment (the marginal efficiency of capital), and government capital expenditures (net exports added).

Ferber (1953, p. 12) has suggested that the adjustment of consumption functions for population "would seem to constitute a basic criterion of a valid aggregate (consumption) function." In his classification and review of twenty-four consumption functions, twelve had no adjustment for population. He draws attention to the work of Staehle (1937) who suggests that the degree of inequality in the *distribution of labor income approximates the importance of the amount of labor income* (emphasis mine) in wage units in explaining the fluctuations in the ratio of retail sales to labor income. This suggestion is central to the theoretical and empirical work necessary to understand important aspects of economic asymmetry. A significant departure from the Keynesian consumption function occurred with the development of the permanent income hypothesis (Friedman 1957). The permanent income hypothesis maintains that the consumption of the household or individual depends on its (or his/her) expectation of income and wealth to be derived over a lifetime. In this view, the individual holds his wealth intact while consuming a relatively constant proportion of the present value of income flowing from work and wealth holdings. Measured income and measured consumption are comprised of permanent and transitory components. The permanent elements are the planned and anticipated elements of consumption. The transitory elements are gains of losses of income and unanticipated changes in consumption. Individuals consume a constant proportion of their permanent income over the long run. A significant proportion of households/individuals experience a declining component of income over the business cycle which results in an increase in their average propensity to consume. This set of conditions gives rise to the short-run consumption function.

With this approach, there are significant issues related to the estimation of values for permanent income and consumption. The purchase of consumer durables is distinguished as investment by the individual/household, while only the flow of services from the purchase of durables is counted as consumption. This factor, and distinguishing between permanent and transitory income represent complex measurement issues.

Another variant of the permanent-income hypothesis is the life-cycle hypothesis presented by Modigliani and Brumberg (1954). The life-cycle theory assumes that an individual consumes a constant proportion of the present value of their lifetime income during each period of their income producing years. They suggest that the long run consumption function captures this effect. The distribution of these consumption expenditures is a matter of the individual's tastes and preferences. However, because the distribution of the population by age and income is relatively constant, the individual consumption functions can be aggregated to produce an overall consumption function. The life-cycle hypothesis is based on the following model (Ruby 2002) (see Table 7.2).

This theoretical approach is an effort to specify a consumption function based on the lifetime earnings of the *average* individual (emphasis mine). This argument is based on the empirical observations that a random sample of individual/households would reveal disproportionate shares of young or old individuals at the lower end of the income distribution and disproportionate shares of middle age individuals at the upper end of the income distribution.

This theory suggests that young and old households have a higher-than-average propensity to consume and may even be engaged in over spending. The young may borrow against future earnings, whereas the old may spend-down their life savings. Comparatively, with middle-aged individuals/households either pay off accumulated debt or save for old age. These conditions affect the average propensities to consume for the three groups. Individual/

TABLE 7.2: The Lifecycle Hypothesis

$\max U_t = \Sigma^L[U(C_t)(1-\delta)^{-t}]$ where
$\max U_t$ = maximization of utility from consumption over time
$U(C_t)$ = satisfaction received from consumption in time period t
C_t = level of consumption over time
δ = the rate of time preference between present and future activity
W_O = initial level of income-producing assets
Y = income
L = lifetime of consumer
N = Number of years with income
$(1+r)^{-t}$ = discount term

During a person's lifetime, consumption must equal income:
$\Sigma^L(C_t)(1+r)^{-t} = \Sigma^N Y_t(1+r)^{-t} + W_O$

household income rises or falls over the business cycle, and these long-run averages of income create a short-run consumption function.

The permanent-income hypothesis and the life-cycle hypothesis highlight important observations for this paper. The consumption function is affected by the fact that incomes are distributed at low average levels for younger- and older-aged individuals, at higher average values for those who are middle-aged.

Seater (1998) has observed that there have been a number of empirically based rejections of the permanent-income and life-cycle hypothesis models. He suggests that these models have been rejected because of the characteristics of the aggregate data or from model misspecifications. He has suggested that reformulating of the consumption function will provide more accurate results.

POSSIBLE SYNTHESIS

This dispute sets the stage for the beginning of the synthesis proposed in this research. This synthesis is constructed from the disparate background presented in this introduction. Initially, there is the consumption function suggested by Keynes (1936), which reappears in different forms (for example, Modigliani and Brumberg 1954, Friedman 1957). Central to this research is the determination of how variation in demographic conditions affects or constrains personal consumption.

Keynes maintains that levels of consumption depend on "effective demand" which is the consequence of levels of personal income subtracting out taxes and moderated by the individual's/household's marginal propensity to consume and marginal propensity to save. Modigliani and Brumberg (1954) add a more detailed perspective by bringing to the fore the nature of income distributions by *age groupings* (emphasis mine).

Kuznets (1966) added his perspective to this call for disaggregation as a path to better understanding economic growth. Kuznets (1966) has maintained that the *different impact of population growth on distinct economic groups within a nation merits further analysis* (emphasis mine). He did not suggest what those units of analysis and the detailed nature of that analysis might be.

An obvious, but somewhat overlooked, fact is that levels of personal income from all sources both allow and constrain personal consumption. The importance of this condition is made more evident by Creamer's (1956) finding that "variation in personal income levels corresponds on a one-to-one basis with the variation of business cycles." Thus, the examination of conceptual or theoretical variables related to variations in personal income is a focus of this research.

Understandings of variations in personal income are enhanced by the understandings initially developed by Schultz (1964) and Becker (1975). Their addition of the value of education, experience and training as *human capital* (emphasis mine) to economic growth and well-being contributed to understanding its role in promoting economic growth. Denison (1962, 1974) empirically assessed the role of the "quality" of labor in economic growth in the United States. His analysis was later used for comparative purposes by Kuznets (1966). Kuznets (1966, 1973) developed estimates of the proportionate role of the human factor and the *quality of labor* (emphasis mine) in modern economic growth within the United States and across a selection of developed nations.

Importantly, there were unexplained residuals in efforts to explain economic growth. Kuznets (1966) found through his empirical deductions that about one-third of the rate of growth was unaccounted for and called this "residual efficiency." Whereas Solow concentrated on the role of labor and capital in the growth of output, the Solow residual appears to account for approximately 50 per cent of the growth in the private economy from 1874 to 1950 (Blanchard and Fischer 1998).

Keynes in his Galton Lecture to the *Eugenics Society* (1937) has offered additional insights for those interested in understanding some aspects of economic asymmetry. In this speech, Keynes notes the expectation of continuing population growth (in the developed world—comment mine) is not a given. He acknowledged that the time lag effects of vital statistics can be observed.

Population decline is one such possibility. He stated, "An era of increasing population tends to promote optimism." In an era of declining population demand, which tends to be based on current rather than future conditions, a state of over-supply is likely to occur. Demand for capital declines in the situation of a declining population. The demand for capital becomes dependent on the increase or decrease in the average level of consumption. There are increased demands for a growing population. In summary, Keynes states "a phase of declining population will make it immensely more difficult than before to maintain prosperity."

A related viewpoint was generalized by Staehle (1937) who has suggested that the distribution of incomes from earnings ranks in importance with the amount of incomes from earnings in its usefulness in explaining variations in the ratio of retail sales to labor income. An additional aspect of economic asymmetry is the study of asymmetries in information. Riley (2001) has reviewed this literature. Of most relevance is the work of Shapiro and Stiglitz (1984); they propose an information-based explanation of unemployment. An employee's wage exceeds the wage level that makes him indifferent to staying on a job. Employers observe employees to ensure that their work effort is maintained. If they do not maintain a satisfactory level of work effort then the employee is fired and is at risk of having wages lower than his former wage. This optimizing behavior of employer and employee is the source of equilibrium unemployment. This view accounts for the efforts of employees to maintain employment.

In more recent research on business cycles, Diebold and Rudebusch (1999) have maintained that evidence of "duration dependence" of business cycles is important in understanding macroeconomic variations. They restate earlier findings and offer six *general* conclusions about the nature and occurrence of expansions and contractions. They have searched for mathematical techniques and application methods to predict turning points and switching behavior of the business cycle. They have documented the United States Commerce Department's Composite Coincident Index which closely monitors the business cycle for the 1952.1–1993.1 period. Of interest to this research are the four component indices (personal income minus transfer payments, an index of industrial production, manufacturing and trade sales, and employees on nonagricultural payrolls) that were suggested to be evidence of a common factor underlying economic activity. The presence of common turning points or switching times for these four quantities is taken by Diebold and Rudebusch (1999) to be suggestive of some underlying model or factor. They question the application of nonlinear models in light of the success of linear models and proceed to suggest and test (with mixed results) some alternative models.

RELEVANT DATA

Of importance to this theoretical presentation is what appears to be the primary importance of the four component indices of the United States Commerce Department's Composite Coincident Index. When compared to the NBER's dating process for business cycles, the similarity of the four measures permits narrowing the focus to what is important to understanding the empirical dynamics of economic fluctuations. The observations and documentation provided by Creamer (1956) suggest that understanding the dynamics of personal income represents a worthwhile focus for the development of an inductively based theoretical framework. Second, the theoretical underpinning of Keynesian economics suggests the primary role of effective demand or personal consumption. Personal income is both an enabling and constraining factor on personal consumption. The understanding that personal consumption represents approximately 69 per cent of the United States' economic activity provides further incentive for trying to understand both theoretically and empirically the nexus of personal income and personal consumption and their influence on economic variations.

The resolution of how demographic change affects economic asymmetry is, however, more complex than concentrating on singular aspects of the dynamics in an economic system. Defining the economic changes in non-homogeneous societies due to: changing population numbers, age groups with changing incomes, changing human capital, or quality of labor levels; changing mixes of sex, age, and ethnicity requires a theoretical view that permits integration of these and other aspects of individual participation in an economy. This research addresses these issues in Chapter 8.

CHAPTER 8

Explaining Business Cycles

INTRODUCTION AND BACKGROUND

The efforts of economists to understand business cycles have extended back over 100 years. The writing of Wesley C. Mitchell (1913) was an example. Over 1,400 books have been written on the subject (Questia.com). The author has relied on and will reference three that have been essential to his research on the subject. They are Keynes's Galton Lecture on declining population (1937), Kuznets's (1979) study of population, capital, and growth, and more recently Janovich and Siu's (2007) study of demographics and business cycle volatility.

Keynes in his Galton Lecture to the *Eugenics Society* (1937) has offered insights for those interested in understanding some aspects of economic asymmetry. In this speech, Keynes notes an expectation of continuing population growth was not a given. He acknowledged that the time lag effects of vital statistics can be observed. Population decline was one such possibility. He stated "An era of increasing population tends to promote optimism." In an era of declining population demand, which tends to be based on current rather than future conditions, a state of oversupply was likely to occur. Demand for capital declines in the situation of a declining population. The demand for capital becomes dependent on the increase or decrease in the average level of consumption. There are increased demands for a growing population. In summary, Keynes states "a phase of declining population will make it immensely more difficult than before to maintain prosperity."

Kuznets (1979) has analyzed the relationship between population growth and *per capita* income for 21 developed nations from the early 1950's to 1964 and finds a negative Spearman correlation (r = -.434). However, when four countries that had populations with higher growth rates than those of Europe or Japan were removed, the Spearman correlation became r = .061. Kuznets quantitative efforts are limited by the lack of data necessary to cover important structural divisions in the economy. Kuznets suggests:

> Both the effects of population increase on aspects of economic growth other than aggregate income per capita and the differential impact of population growth on distinct subcategories within a country obviously merit further analysis. (p. 48)

This statement was followed by an observation relevant to this research: the changing levels of population growth and decline alter the number of consumer and income receiving equivalent units.

Kuznets (1979) states that 'material capital stock effectively increases output *only* if it was supplemented by some uses of product now classified as *consumption*" (p. 25) (emphasis mine). Consumption and all forms of personal income are important in the occurrence of periods of economic asymmetry.

Jaimovich and Siu (2007) found that demographic (age) change accounted for a significant amount of business cycle volatility in international panel (G7) data. The data permitted them to analyze the age composition of the labor force as a significant contributor to business cycle variation. While their work concentrated on the volatility of employment by age group (and thus wages and salaries) it does not include participation in government programs such as Social Security, Unemployment Compensation, Social Security Disability, public welfare, Black Lung Benefits, and so forth.

The Keynesian and Monetarist approaches agree that variations in aggregate demand create business cycles. The two schools of thought disagree on the causes of these variations. For Keynesians the sources are variable expectations due to volatility in investment and consumption. Changes in investment and consumption effect swings in aggregate output. Monetarists believe wages and prices are perfectly flexible. Aggregate supply determines output in the long-run and changes in aggregate demand affect supply in the short-run. The Rational Expectation s Model asserts that unexpected changes in policy have effects on output (Taylor, 1985).

In summation, shocks such as tornadoes, tsunamis, earthquakes, 9/11, and war are important because of their effects on supply and/or demand. Globalization of the economy, trade agreements, housing demand, and banking crises are contributors to economic disruption and to fall in demand or declining wages. The summary effects of shocks or changes in supply and/or demand are mirrored in the variables selected for this analysis (ethnicity, sex, age group, numbers with income by subcategory and mean income by subcategory). Shocks affect demand and/or supply either directly or indirectly.

METHOD, VARIABLES, AND DATA

The general method used in this research was to compare two different methods of calculating personal income to each other (I) qualitatively and (II) quantitatively. The reason for using personal income was that the National Bureau of Economic Research's Dating Committee—uses personal income to measure the beginning and ends of business cycles. The first method used in calculating personal income was using the NIPA as the standard. This method calculates various economic variables (including personal income) using a double entry accounting system. In this method, every payment and receipt for goods or services was recorded for each major element of the national chart of accounts. The second method specified personal income by calculations from (a) the CPS using income by ethnicity, sex, age group, number in the group with income, and average income of the group (1967–2000). A second set of calculations (b) used income by ethnicity, sex, number in the group with income, and average income (1967–2011) of the group. The results were then compared to NIPA results in two different ways. Each CPS data series and calculation (a, b) of total estimated personal income was compared quantitatively and figuratively to the NIPA personal income data as well as graphically to the National Bureau of Economic Research's dating of recessions.

First, it was expected that NIPAPI (National Income and Product Accounts personal income) and ESTPINC (CPS, ASEC estimated personal income, 1967–2000, (N=34) were highly correlated.

Second, that ESTPINC2 was significantly correlated to the dependent variable NIPAPI (N = 45).

The central argument of this paper was that the number in the population with categorical characteristics of ethnicity, sex, age subcategory, mean income by subcategory, and the number having income, explain economic expansions and contractions (ultimately the variation of live births by subcategory cohort, the pattern of subcategory cohort aging and decline, and the subcategory mean income of those with income at time t).

The variables used were defined so they were mutually exclusive. The subcategories used are included in Table 8.1.

The variation in live births and survivorship by defined subcategory over time becomes translated into variable numbers of surviving numbers in each subcategory and fewer of those individuals with income. This was made true by the highly variable nature of birth levels by subgroup, changing male-female proportions, differences in the numbers of individuals in each subcategory of child-producing ages, differences in birthrates by subcategory, and differences in survival patterns. These and other variations get translated, in part, into variation over time in the numbers with personal income having the unique subcategories of ethnicity, sex, age, number with income, and mean money income.

There are four sources of the data used in this research: first, the Current Population Survey (CPS), March Annual Social and Economic Supplement (ASEC) 1967–2000; second, the Current Population Survey (CPS), March Annual Social and Economic Supplement (ASEC) 1967–2011; the National Bureau of Economic Research Dating Procedures; and the National Income and Product Accounts (NIPA) (see references).

A paper detailing the first and second data options was Design, and Methodology, Technical Paper TP63RV, written by the Department of Labor.

The Bureau of Census, Income Survey Branch asks questions about the amount of money received in a preceding calendar year. From these (CPS, ASEC) sources of statistics, the data are prepared into sets of tables identified by sex, ethnicity, age, number with income, and mean personal income by subcategory.

The CPS, ASEC income data did not include capital gains and was taken before Social Security, income taxes, union dues, Social Security Disability income, public welfare, and Medicare are taken out. Income does not count consumption due to the accumulation of debt. It does not reflect that some individuals receive their income in the form of non-cash benefits such as food stamps, health benefits, reduced housing costs, business perks, or home-produced goods or services. A weakness of the ASEC at the high-end of income was that those responding who have categorically $150,000 or more dollars have their total income estimated. Currently (since 2009), those individuals who declare 250,000 dollars of money income have money income estimated.

The CPS evolved from its assignment to the Bureau of the Census in 1943 through a wide variety of changes culminating in the CPS in 2001. The CPS sample was a multi-stage random stratified sample that has evolved with areas in each state being sampled. It features a March Annual Social and Economic Supplement (ASEC) from which money income data, demographics, and persons with income were drawn for this research.

Of central importance to this theoretical and empirical presentation was Creamer's (1956) work on Personal Income. The observations and documentation by Creamer (1956) suggest that understanding the dynamics of personal income represents a worthwhile focus for developing a deductively based theoretical framework for business cycles. Second, the theoretical underpinning of Keynesian economics (1936) suggests the primary role of

TABLE 8.1: Population, Number with Personal Income, and Mean Personal Income for 2000 by Ethnicity, Age, and Sex (2000 current dollars)

Ethnic & Age subcategory	Population	Number with Personal Income	Mean Personal Income	Ethnic & Age subcategory	Population	Number with Personal Income	Mean Personal Income
White Non-Hispanic Males			$	Hispanic Males			$
15–24	13,002,127	10,226,000	13,666	15–24	2,933,485	2,016,000	13,800
25–34	12,518,851	11,979,000	41,539	25–34	2,722,095	2,711,000	27,056
35–44	16,226,416	15,737,000	54,461	35–44	2,519,989	2,481,000	31,982
45–54	14,112,168	14,080,000	59,919	45–54	1,517,684	1,472,000	33,012
55–64	9,200,538	8,707,000	54,901	55–64	813,997	833,000	28,046
65 plus	12,134,022	11,672,000	31,211	65 plus	816,647	737,000	17,223
White Non-Hispanic Females				Hispanic Females			
15–24	12,329,839	9,727,000	11,244	15–24	2,716,205	1,702,000	10,111
25–34	12,553,785	11,399,000	25,867	25–34	2,594,060	2,201,000	19,026
35–44	16,190,407	15,055,000	29,343	35–44	2,422,200	2,051,000	19,381
45–54	14,383,623	13,796,000	30,215	45–54	1,586,206	1,393,000	21,512
55–64	9,804,961	9,068,000	23,658	55–64	945,903	744,000	17,281
65 plus	16,963,405	15,246,000	16,414	65 plus	1,120,943	989,000	10,047
African-American Males			$	Other Males			$
15–24		1,649,000	10,817	15–24	946,781	677,000	12,209
25–24	2,343,633	2,086,000	33,145	25–24	973,348	1,151,000*	39,539
35–44	2,533,454	2,501,000	33,043	35–44	1,009,266	1,096,000*	56,782
45–54	1,790,106	1,834,000	33,483	45–54	754,139	821,000*	53,264
55–64	999,232	977,000	35,595	55–64	429,385	421,000	45,336
65 plus	1,111,755	1,076,000	20,090	65 plus	410,441	474,000*	22,370
African-American Females				Other Females			
15–24	2,758,273	2,012,000	10,282	15–24	950,396	663,000	11,658
25–34	2,613,931	2,643,000	22,705	25–34	1,120,773	1,034,000	26,507
35–44	2,882,745	2,890,000	25,06235–44		1,109,290	1,081,000	26,469
45–54	2,160,723	2,162,000	28,13545–54		861,553	840,000	26,249
55–64	1,315,793	1,207,000	20,38855–64		491,287	416,000	23,553
65 plus	1,715,030	1,612,000	12,341	65 plus	563,050	511,000	13,274

*numbers with personal income > population are excessive. They are derived values and their ratio should not exceed .99. Source: Current Population Survey (CPS), Annual Social and Economic Supplement (ASEC). It should be noted that the category for Hispanics did not exist from 1967–1972. Hispanics were counted as Whites.

effective demand and personal consumption. Personal income was both an enabling and constraining factor on personal consumption. The understanding that personal consumption represents approximately 69 per cent of U.S. annual economic activity provides further reason to try to understand both theoretically and empirically the nexus of personal income and personal consumption and their influence on economic variations.

This research now addresses these issues.

THE CONTEXT AND CHANGES IN COHORT SIZE

The number of individuals in a particular ethnic, sex, age, mean income, and money income group and factors influencing their status can be classified into three categories.

It was important to note that as cohorts of live births age they decline in size (see Figure 8.1). The cohort of live births has an important effect on what happens in the future beyond the birth date or birth year. The composition of the cohort and its duration are part of what affects personal income.

TABLE 8.2: Antecedent, Contextual, and Present Factors Affecting Average Personal Income

Antecedent	Contextual	Present (per time of ASEC data collection)
Factors affecting live births Live births by category Ethnicity, sex, time of birth, place of birth genetics	Survival pattern, social-economic-status, wage structure, education, supply, international labor markets, living arrangements, level of unionization, automation, other environmental factors such as trade agreements	Ethnicity[1,2,3] Sex[1,2,3], age group [1,2], mean income[1,2,3] Average money income by group[1,2,3] Those with money income[1,2,3]

[1,2,3] Used in Part I of the analysis; [1,2] used in part I and II of the analysis

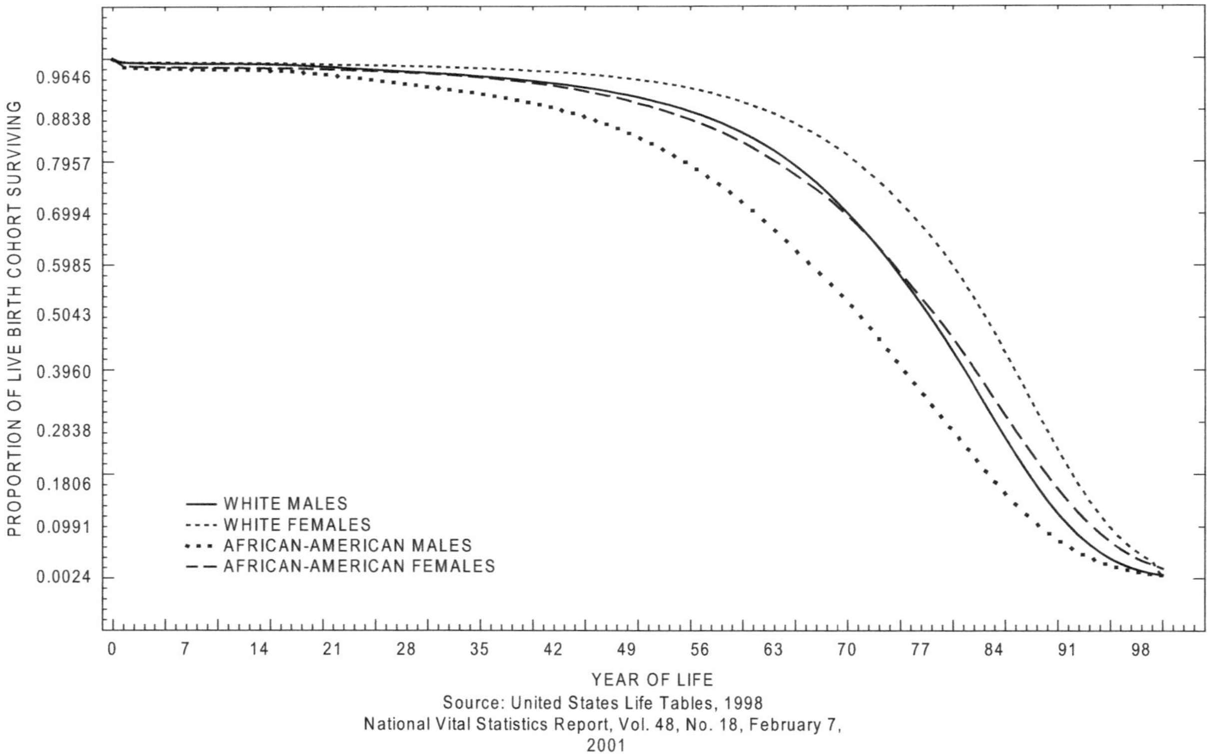

FIGURE 8.1: Proportion of Live Birth Cohort Surviving in Each year of Life, White Males, White Females, African-American Males, and African –American Females, 1998

Each year of data for the variables in Table 8.1 was developed as annual panel data. For Part I there were 34 annual panels created with the noted exception for Hispanics in 1967–1972. For purposes of simplification only White Non-Hispanic Male and Female data for 2000 was presented in Table 8.1. One table was developed for each year (1967–2000; N=34). Data from the CPS ASEC from 1967–2000 was aggregated into total personal income and analyzed. The 1967–2011 data came from the CPS, ASEC. The latter period consisted of males and females broken down by White, Black, Hispanic, and Other. Two levels of analysis were done because of differences in the composition of the data. The first analysis was done by the analysis of demographic variables from 1967–2000. The second analysis was done with slightly different data excluding age groups from 1967 to 2011.

An important question was now understood by observing the 45 tables. What are some important sources of variation in personal income?

There are six general conditions that could contribute prominently to the variation in *total or aggregate* current dollar personal income. These are: (1) the number of individuals in the population of a subcategory by, (2) sex, (3) age subcategory, (4) ethnicity, (5) the number with income in each subcategory, and (6) the level of mean income by subcategory. All are conditions that vary with time. It was important to realize that this does not include variables at an intermediate or tertiary level which affected the variables (1) through (6).

DEVELOPING THE BASIS FOR CALCULATING PERSONAL INCOME AND PERSONAL CONSUMPTION

Kuznets's (1979) insights on the relevance of population growth to consumption, Keynes' article (1937) on the effect of declining population on consumption, and Jaimovich and Siu's article (2007) finding that change in age groups accounted for some business cycle volatility stimulated the line of inquiry that follows.

First, and most prominent, was the fact that personal consumption (PC) accounts for slightly over 69 per cent of the variation in aggregate demand. Knowledge that PC was such an important part of economic activity helps us to understand the sources of that activity.

$$\sum_{x=1}^{x=n} PC_{XT} = \sum_{x=1}^{x=n} ((\overline{PI}_{XT} - (\overline{tx}_{xt} \pm \overline{s}_{xt} \pm \overline{db}_{xt})) \quad (8.1)$$

$\overline{PI}_{XT}$ = mean personal income of group x at time t

$\overline{tx}_{xt}$ = mean taxes of group x at time t

$\overline{s}_{xt}$ = mean savings of group x at time t (net deposits or withdrawals)

$\overline{db}_{xt}$ = debt of group x at time t (net debt acquisition or payments)

PC_{XT} = personal consumption of group x at time t

$group_{xt}$ x = 1,2, 3…n at time t

To obtain total personal income, the number of individuals with personal income in each subgroup (NPY_x) at a given time was multiplied by the average personal income for each population subgroup. The totals for each subgroup are then added to get ESTPINC and ESTPINCII.

$$(NPY_{xt})(\overline{Y}_{xt}) = GRPY_{xt} \quad (8.2)$$

$\overline{Y}_{xt}$ = mean personal income for group x at time t

NPY_{xt} = number with personal income for group x at time t

$GRPY_{xt}$ = total group personal income for all groups x. x= 1, 2, …n at time t, t=1,2…m

X_t = group identified by sex, age, ethnicity, possessing income, and mean income . x = 1, 2…n, t=1, 2…m

Once $GRPY_{xT}$ was calculated for each x and t, the results can be summed to determine the estimated total personal income (ESTPINC).

$$ESTPINC_t = \sum_{x=1}^{x=m} GRPY_{xt} \quad (8.3)$$

The numbers of people receiving personal income and their mean personal incomes varies by sex, age, and ethnicity in the data from the Current Population Survey website (the Annual Social and Economic Supplement). It was important to note that the selected categories in Table 8.1 allow clear distinctions between different groups of the income-receiving population. However, other categorizations are also possible. Specifically, if data were available in combination with other variables, education level could be used as another characteristic upon which categories could be based. Two problems in searching for data were that it was not mutually exclusive or was not available.

VARIATION IN THE POPULATION BY SEX, AGE AND ETHNIC SUBCATEGORY

Figure 8.2 shows how the numbers in each white, male, Non-Hispanic age group have varied and will vary over the future from 1976 to 2015. Use of the total population hides the variations in the subgroup size. This variation in subgroup size combined with levels of mean income receipt, sex, age differences, and differences in ethnicity to delineate variation in total personal income.

ANALYSIS PART 1

The presentations of qualitative and quantitative analytical approaches follow. To verify the usefulness of estimated total personal income ESTPINC (Figure 8.3) was compared to the National Bureau of Economic Research's (NBER) Dating Committee's timing of recessions (Table 8.3) taken from the Department of Commerce quarterly NIPA personal income statistics. One of the limitations of this approach was that the data used for ESTPINC are annual and the data used by the NBER Dating Committee are quarterly.

For comparison, a figure of estimated total personal income derived from the Current Population Survey (CPS), Annual Social and Economic Supplement (ASEC) (see Figure 8.3) and was presented with an overlay of the percentage change from year-to-year. Downturns in the dotted line represent periods of economic downturn. To verify the usefulness of estimated total personal income, ESTPINC2 (Figure 8.4) was compared to the National Bureau of Economic Research's (NBER) Dating Committee's timing of recessions (Table 8.3) taken from the Bureau of Census, CPS, ASEC annual

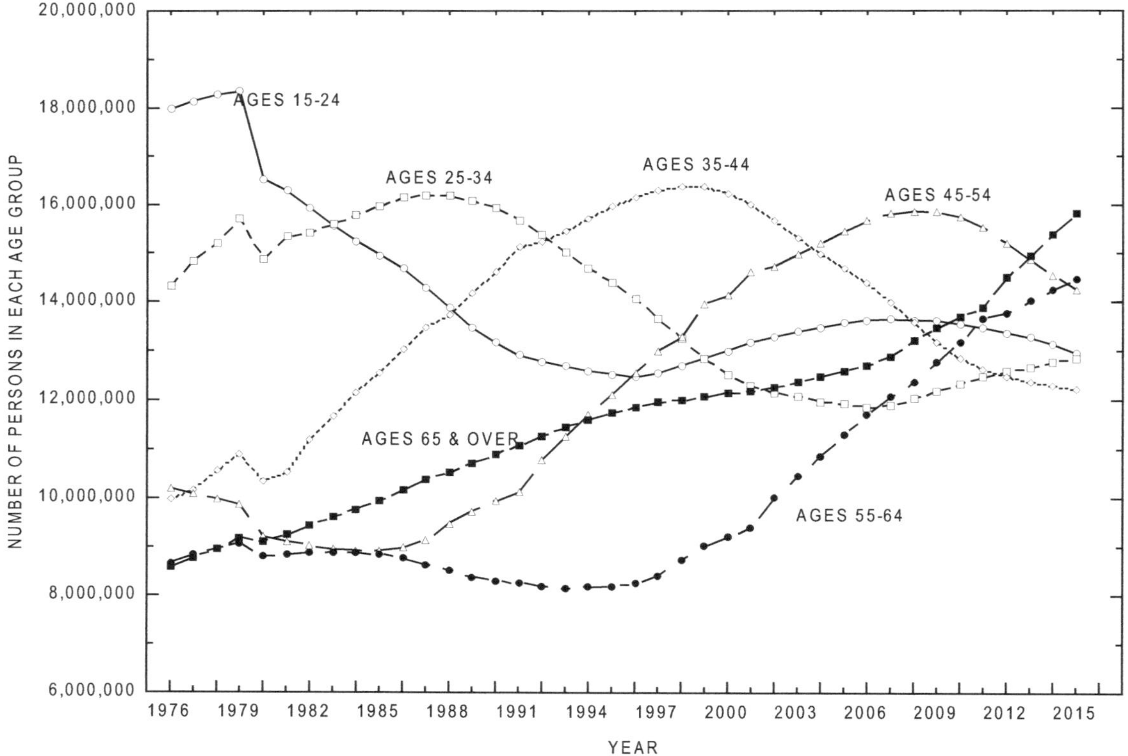

FIGURE 8.2: Number of White, Non-Hispanic Males by Age Subcategories 1976–2015

TABLE 8.3: BUSINESS CYCLES

REFERENCE DATES		DURATION IN MONTHS	
Peak	**Trough**	**Cycle**	**Trough**
		Peak from Previous Peak	**Match**
December 1969 (IV)	November 1970 (IV)	116	Yes
November 1973 (IV)	March 1975 (I)	47	Yes
January 1980 (I)	July 1980 (III)	74	Yes
July 1981 (III)	November 1982 (IV)	18	Yes
July 1990 (III)	March 1991 (I)	108	Yes
March 2001 (I)	November 2001 (IV)	128	Yes
December 2007 (IV)	June 2009 (II)	81	Yes

NBER Dating Committee Data Compared to ESTPINC2 (Figure 8.4)

personal income statistics. Again, one of the limitations of this approach was that the data used for ESTPINC2 were annual and the data from the NBER Dating Committee were quarterly.

A second figure was prepared. Figure 8.3 shows a match of the annual decreases that represent percentage changes and peaks and troughs in personal income with the National Bureau of Economic Research Dating Committee's dates for peaks and troughs from 1967 through 2011.

Figure 8.3 and Figure 8.4 show a match of the annual decreases and represent percentage changes in personal income with the National Bureau of Economic Research Dating Committee's dates for peaks and troughs from 1967 through 2000 and 1967 through 2011 respectively.

The similarity of the troughs specified by the National Bureau of Economic Research Dating Committee and the estimated troughs from the CPS ASEC data are qualitative proof of the value of CPS, ASEC data subcategories in explaining business cycles.

To repeat this analysis one must go to the original CPS data.

ANALYSIS PART 2

The following variables were used in the analysis for periods of thirty-four (34) and forty-five (45) years.

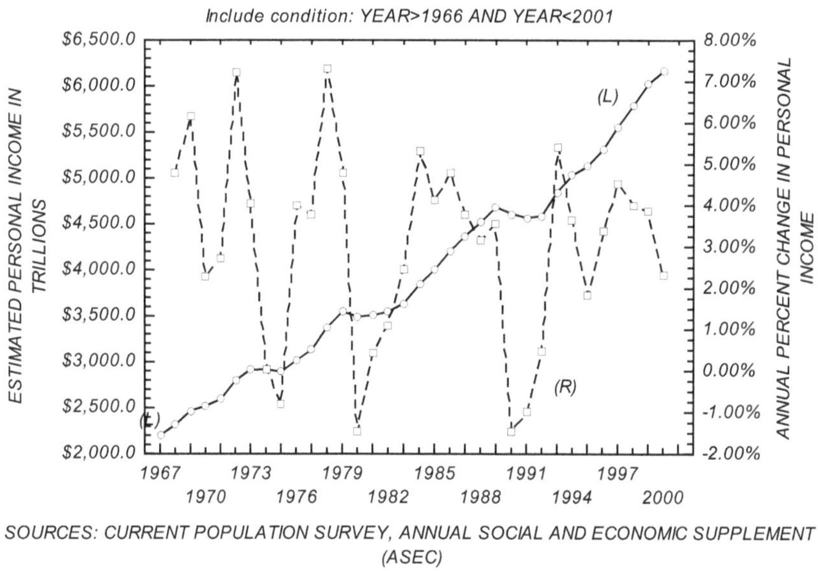

FIGURE 8.3: Estimated Personal Income (ESTPINC), and Estimated Annual Percent Change in Personal Income

NIPAPI—personal income in the United States (US) in current dollars from the National Income and Product Accounts

NIPAPIDIFF—personal income in the US lagged and differenced from the National Income and Product Accounts.

ESTPINC—estimated personal income using 36 categories from 1967–1972 and 48 categories thereafter to 2000. Income and mean income were sub-categories associated with ethnicity, sex, and age. Estimated personal income (ESTPINC) from 1967 to 2000 was based on the March Current Population Supplement (ASEC). It was based on the categories and subcategories above. The period of 1967–2011 was based on the same categories and subcategories, but age was not included. This variable was ESTPINC2.

USUNEMP—the number of unemployed persons in the US in thousands (Bureau of Labor Statistics)

An important question was what are the ways that NIPAPI, ESTPINC, NIPAPIDIFF, and ESTPINC2 should be analyzed? The purpose was to prove that the pairs of variables (NIPAPI and ESTPINC, and NIPAPIDIFF

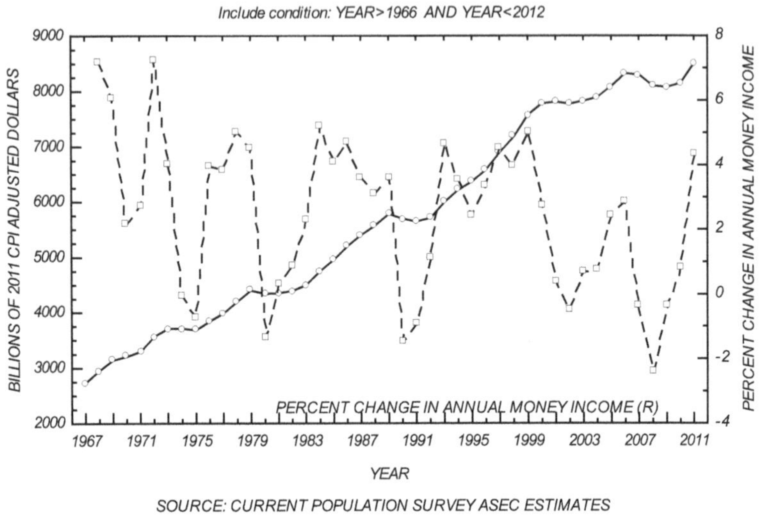

FIGURE 8.4: Estimated Money Income in 2011 Dollars (L) and Annual Percent Change (R)

and ESTPINC, NIPAPI and ESTPINC2, and NIPAPIDIFF and ESTPINC2) are highly similar and reflect the variation due to business cycles and recessions at similar times in the course of time.

Thirty-four panels of data each containing 48 subcategories (except for Hispanics from 1967–1972), were converted into a longitudinal series for each subcategory. The subcategories were used to calculate yearly total personal income for each ethnic, sex, and age subcategory. The subcategories were collapsed by addition into year and ethnic groups (see previously stated mathematical notations). Each ethic group was added into annual personal income for the group and then into total annual personal income for all groups. While the methods used were calculation intensive, that was necessary to understand the phenomenon. The method used was very similar to that of the Index of Consumer Sentiment which was conducted by the Survey Research Center at the University of Michigan. Panel data are collected for each period. This was converted into aggregate data. A time series was created by sequencing the respective annual data points.

The purpose was to show that the end result of constructing the variables ESTPINC and ESTPINC2 results in variables that mimic the behavior of the variable NIPA for two different time periods as correlated and dependent variables.

TABLE 8.4: Correlation Matrix, N=34

	UNEMP	NIPAPI	NIPAPIDIFF
NIPAPI	.36**	--	
NIPAPIDIFF	.30***	.90*	--
ESTPINC	.34**	.999*	.90*

* = p= .00, **<.05, *** not significant

An important question was what are the ways that NIPAPI, ESTPINC, NIPAPIDIFF, and ESTPINC2 should be analyzed? The purpose was to show that the pairs of variables (ESTPINC and NIPAPI, ESTPINC2 and NIPAPIDIFF) are highly similar and reflect the variation due to business cycles and recessions at similar times. The purpose was to show that the end result of constructing the variables ESTPINC AND ESTPINC2 results in variables that mimic the behavior of the variable NIPA despite their being derived by totally different methods.

The statistical methods available to analyze pairs of variables are limited. It was determined that correlation analysis, linear regression analysis, and multiple regression analysis of dependent and independent variables would be used for relationships in this analysis.

First a linear regression analysis (Table 8.6) was conducted in which NIPAPI was the dependent variable and ESTPINC (N=34) was the independent variable (equation 8.1). In equation 8.2, NIPAPIDIFF, the independent variable, was estimated using estimated personal income (ESTPINC) as the independent variable.

In equation 1 the correlation of NAPI and ESTPINC was high at .99. In equation 2 the correlation of NIPADIFF and ESTPINC was r=.90. In

TABLE 8.5: Means and Standard Deviations, N =34

	Means	Standard Deviations
UNEMP	6800.15	2007.54
NIPAPI	3536.14	2364.47
NIPAPIDIFF	233.99	137.22
ESTPINC	2421.56	1660.45

TABLE 8.6: Linear Regression Results, 1967–2000

	Variable	b	Std. Error of b	t	p
(Eq 1)	NIPAPI				
	Intercept	-4654.94	211.36	-22.02	0.00
	ESTPINC	2.08	0.05	40.26	0.00
r=.99, F=1620.9, p=0.00, SEE =334.09, s.c. = .69, N=34					
(Eq 2)	NIPAPIDIFF				
	Intercept	203.31	36.37	-5.59	0.00
	ESTPINC	0.111	0.008	16.49	0.00
r =.90, F=156.04, p<0.00, SEE=57.49, s.c. = .10, N =34					

equation 1 the serial correlation was high, indicating multicollinearity. In equation 2, the serial correlation was low and indicates a low level of multicollinearity. In these relationships both of the correlation coefficients are significant at p = 0.00

ANALYSIS PART 3

To extend the analysis, a different data set with a larger N (N=45) was used. Data were not available in the same form as in Part I of the analysis. To conduct the analysis a spreadsheet of data that featured five variables were used [(source Current Population Survey, ASEC (1967–2011): There are five general conditions that could contribute prominently to the variation in *total or aggregate* current dollar personal income. These are: (1) the number of individuals in the population of a subcategory by (2) ethnicity, (3) sex, (4) the number with income in each subcategory, and (5) the mean income level of the subcategory. Age was not included. All are conditions that vary with time. The data were in 2011 Current Price Index terms and were deflated. The 1992 CPI deflator was used. This resulted in the variable ESTPINC2 [estimated personal or money income (1967–2011)].

Thus, 45 panels of data each containing 48 subcategories, (except for Hispanics from 1967–1972), were converted into a longitudinal series for each subcategory. The subcategories were used to calculate yearly total personal income for each ethnic, and sex subcategory. The subcategories were collapsed by addition into year and ethnic groups. Each ethic group was added into annual personal income for the group and then into total annual personal income for all groups. The methods used were calculation intensive. The method used in calculating estimated personal income (ESTPINC2) was similar to that in Part II used to calculate ESTPINC with the exception that age was not used as a subcategory.

Multiple regression analysis of dependent and independent variables for relationships were used in this analysis.

The correlation coefficients preliminary to the linear regression analysis are in Table 8.7.

The correlations in Table 8.7 are harbingers of what the results of the multiple regression equations 3 and 4 are in Table 8.9.

The two regression equations (see Table 8.9) have two characteristics in common. The t values are significant for each independent variable. The p values are significant for each independent variable. There was autocorrelation in equation 3. The F values for all equations are significant at p = 0.00. The Standard Error of Estimate was smaller in equation 4 than in equation 3. The Durbin-Watson Statistic in equation 3 indicates there was autocorrelation present. In equation 4, the Durbin-Watson Statistic shows no auto correlation present.

There is an important contrast between equation (3) and equation (4). Most importantly the Durbin-Watson statistic in equation (3) indicates there is autocorrelation present. Equation (4) is free of autocorrelation.

CONCLUSIONS AND SUMMARY

This paper posits and confirms the assumption that business cycles are the result of irregular causes. Personal income was used as a surrogate for

TABLE 8.7: **Correlation Matrix, N=45**

	UNEMP	NIPAPI	NIPAPIDIFF
NIPAPI	.56*	--	
NIPAPIDIFF	.06**	.53*	--
ESTPINC	2.56*	.998*	.98*

* p= .00, ** not significant

TABLE 8.8: Means and Standard Deviations, N =45

	Mean	Standard Deviation
UNEMP	7483.07	2584.26
NIPAPI	5350.00	3883.80
NIPAPIDIFF	274.30	224.87
ESTPINC2	3594.44	2559.94

variation in aggregate demand or Gross Domestic Product as it represents approximately seventy percent of the economy. Personal income is also used by the National Bureau of Economic Research's Dating Committee as a prime indicator of the beginning and end of recessions as well as an indicator of the health of the U.S. economy. Underneath the surface of aggregate population and income data resides the results of variations in live births by sex, age, ethnicity, mean incomes, number with income, and variations in survival rates. In the case of demand or supply shocks, shocks may affect changes in mean income, changes in numbers participating in the economy, and changes in

TABLE 8.9: Multiple Regression Equations, 1967–2011, N=45

	Variable	b	Std. Error of b	t	p
(Eq 3)	NIPAPI				
	Intercept	-277.58	109.44	-2.54	0.02
	ESTPINC2	1.50	0.017	88.65	0.00
	USUNEMP	.034	0.017	2.04	.048

Adjusted R^2=.996, F=5924.6, p=0.00, SEE =236.25, d.w. = .62 (autocorrelation present), N=45

	Variable	b	Std. Error of b	t	p
(Eq 4)	NIPAPIDIFF				
	Intercept	47.61	83.80	1.76	.085
	ESTPINC2	0.066	.013	5.12	0.00
	USUNEMP	-0.032	.013	-2.50	.016

Adjusted R^2=.36, F=13.20, p=0.00, SEE =180.36, d.w. = 1.80 (no autocorrelation), N=45 other demographic characteristics. Structural factors (population subcategories previously set forth) are the immediate antecedent of demand. Analysis of these relationships should be undertaken with close attention to the sources of annual estimated personal income values and the numbers in each subgroup with income. The truth is that any population subcategories could be used as long as they were mutually exclusive and had mean income, and the number with income as subcategories. The approach suggested here was not an exclusive but is the only one that could be found with available data.

The method presented for explaining ESTPINC expresses what variables are ultimately affected when storms rage, when tsunamis occur, and when earthquakes disturb, when demand declines, when supply increases or drops, and when a number of other intermediate causes occur. The money income or personal income variables for different groups are affected differently.

The lack of quarterly data, comparing annual and quarterly data, and inaccuracies due to this comparison limit the accuracy of these estimates. A second factor to consider is the limitation of CPS, ASEC data at the higher income ranges. Estimates of higher income groups are suspect despite efforts to compensate for limits at the higher end of the income distribution. This manuscript does not address the impact of immigration on population change. This is justified on the basis that immigration spread across age levels will be small in absolute terms compared to the level of surviving live births. Live birth data are expected to include children born in the U.S. to immigrants.

Income defined—Money received in the previous year by each person 15 years and older from the following sources: (1) salary, wages, or self-employment; (2) unemployment compensation; (3) workers' compensation; (4) Social Security; (5) Supplemental Security Income; (6) public assistance; (7) veteran's payments; (8) survivor benefits; (9) pensions; (10) interest and dividends; (11) Rents or royalties or estates or trusts; (12) educational assistance; (13) alimony; (14) child support; (15) gifts and any other periodic or sporadic income; and, (16) tips. Income of persons is all income received by the person from all sources in the previous year.

This paper rejects that business cycles are without causes. Underneath the smooth surface of aggregate population data resides the results of variations in live births, sex, age, ethnicity, mean incomes, and variations in survival rates.

In response to the question the paper began with, I conclude, that this paper has revealed an analytical framework that may be used to anticipate expansions and contractions. Further, at the basis of the findings was the notion that effective demand, most immediately, depends on the number of individuals in ethnic, sex, age, income groups, their mean income, and the number in each subgroup with income. As always, such estimations are only as good as the data used to make them. What has been confirmed is that mean income of groups in the United States by ethnicity, sex and/or age, and those with income can be used to estimate approximate total personal income. The characteristics of the subgroups can be said to be surrogates for other characteristics (e.g. education, survival rates, or more complex forms of ethnicity). In the end, some of what humanity experiences will remain highly random. That will make forecasting difficult.

A major contention of this paper was the fact that total personal income from the National Income and Product Accounts was calculated using a double-entry accounting method can be compared to a method of estimation using ethnicity, sex, (sometimes age), mean income and number with income holds the key to partially understanding what explains business cycles. In fact, the changes in live births, their subcategory characteristics, immigration, their varying survival curves, and shocks or long term trends of many types, globalization of the economy, the decline of unionization, the automation of labor, supply, wage structures, the development of international labor markets, inventories, unemployment, the demand for and pricing of housing, gas prices, and possibly more can all effect personal income in the U.S. The category of estimated personal income and all its subcategories are affected by such factors and movements. Ultimately, any and all of such factors end up affecting total personal income. Total personal income, in turn, has been affected by the intervening variables of ethnicity, sex, age, number with income, and mean income. That's why this paper focuses on total personal income as both a basic and/or an intervening variable that reflects itself in business cycles. Total personal income can be either an intervening variable or a causal variable that was reflected in the peaks and troughs of business cycles.

Confirmation of this methodology was found in the increasing dependency ratio (number 0–14 years + those 65 years and over/those 15 through 64 years of age) in Japan. This was occurring while the population ages and the number 14 years to 64 years decline. In Japan, the dependency ratio will go from .47 in 2005 to .87 in 2040. A similar phenomenon is in its nascent stages in the U.S.

It should be noted that the title off this paper was *Explaining Business Cycles...;* the title was not *The Causes of Business Cycles...* The latter title presumes that the several conditions that affect total personal income, at an intermediate level, are documented with data that can be used to explain time-series causation. Second, the likelihood of ever explaining originating or intermediate causes of business cycles will be difficult. This has been what has made the literature on business cycles so indeterminate. As a result, the task of explaining business cycles will remain fastened on the examination of these demographic effects. This will remain true until it is possible to bring into the analysis data relevant to these originating and intermediate considerations. Such a prospect is daunting and remains unlikely.

In summation, this chapter uses a previous demographic approach to business cycles by expanding it to multiple demographic factors. The conclusions to the paper are (1) business cycles are more complex than causal analysis will allow; (2) the variables closest (in order) to predicting estimated personal income are demographic variables; (3) more remote variables can predict personal income (and therefore business cycles) but the variables do so only through the mediating effects of sex, ethnicity, age, number in group with income, and mean income of each group. Any efforts to explain business cycles in other terms will likely be unsuccessful.

CHAPTER 9

Overview and Alternatives

Data related to graphic analysis, data related to explaining business cycles, verification of variables and their variation as they contribute to economic variation are the source and substance of information necessary to begin to understand the relationship between demographics and the economy. For instance, live births are a rarely used variable in either the field of demographics or economics. Live births, if lagged a specified number of years, represent individuals at the age of the lag plus those that have died. To obtain the number surviving to that age, the number of live births is lagged a specified number of years and then multiplied by the survival rate for the specified age, and sex group. The increase in live births from 1933 to 1960 represented an important period of growth in the U.S. economy with some hiccups along the way. The 1961 through 1975 period represents a period of decline in live births that has had and is having a negative impact on the U.S. economy.

THE CURRENT ECONOMIC CRISIS

The data used for analyzing the economic conditions from 2000 to 2011 and on to 2040 concern the level of live births, survival rates, by sex from 1900 to 2004. These data are collected and prepared by the National Center for Health Statistics and the Social Security Administration. In the case of survival rates that are issued decennially, the survival rates are interpolated to achieve annual survival rates.

Live births from 1933 through 1960 show an annual increase of 3.43 million live births per year. This is a total increase in live births of 93.22 million live births in 27 years. In 1961 there were 4.267 million live births. In 1975 there were 3.144 million live births. That was a total number of 54.54 million live births from 1961 through 1975.

- Male and female live birth levels are lagged by both 45 and 64 years and multiplied by their respective survival rates. Between the lines representing surviving 45 year olds and the line representing 64 year olds there are lags of 46, 47, 48, 49, 50, 51, 52, 53, 54, 55, 56, 57, 58, 59, 60, 61, 62, and 63 years. Thus, the births surviving to 45 and 64 years of age are being used to represent all persons between 45 and 65 years old. There were other reasons that the 45 and 64 year lag were used. It is at the age of 64 to 65 that average income declines. Second, the number of 45 year olds declines in the period from 2006 to 2021.
- From the year 2006 to 2018–2021, the number of individuals will decline to a trough that is four years long . . . the decline in disposable income will extend to 2023 and begin to incline from 2024 on.
- 394 million persons aged 45 years. From 2022 to 2030 there will be 13.474 million persons who are 45 years of age. From 2022 to 2030, there will be 29.453 million persons 64 years of age. From 2022 to 2030, there will be 29.453 million persons 64 years of age. Where are the 45–64 year olds going? They are aging as well as dying.
- The section in Chapter 4 regarding disposable personal income is the author's best estimate of how total disposable personal income and annual change in disposable personal income will respond to both demographic and economic conditions. Given the estimate of disposable personal income and its tendency to increase, by increments of smaller amounts, it will have a difficult time keeping pace with inflation.
- The several ways that the book makes a cogent argument for the nature of the relationship of personal income, disposable personal income, and population to business cycles are there to be tested and, if possible, to be refuted.
- This approach to understanding business cycles places emphasis on the pervasive nature of effective demand as a factor. Policy that focuses on the development of capital for big and small business alike without attending to the levels of effective demand will fail.
- The availability of large amounts of cash in the U.S. is a reflection of the lack of home-based demand. International demand, especially in emerging markets moderates the lack of demand in the U.S. Competition on cost makes U.S. decreases the demand for U.S. products. The survival patterns of live births, their numbers, their sex, their mean income, and their ethnicity results in variation in the total personal income and the total

personal disposable income. As is already evident, the variation in these characteristics has significant effects on personal income, employment-unemployment, and on federal, state, and local revenues.

- The population and income data indicate the current income crisis for low and middle income persons will continue to 2021 and more likely to 2033.
- World economic events, the U.S. debt, political conflict in the U.S., and the domination of the economy and politics by large banks and corporations represent a serious drag on the U.S. economy and government. These factors have not fully calculated into the content and conclusions of this book.

POLICY IMPLICATIONS

- On the revenue side, at the federal level, taxes need to be extended and increased on those eligible to pay taxes on annual incomes of 250,000 dollars and above. Those who profit should be those who pay.
- Corporations and businesses need to be required to pay taxes on all profits above 1 million dollars annually. Deductions and depreciation should be precisely defined. Deductions should not include the destruction of natural resources. Corporate taxes should be instituted and enforced at the national and state levels.
- There was a total decline consisting of 54.54 million live births from 1961 to 1975. This was a mean annual decline of 3.90 million live births.
- The mean total personal income in Chapter I is in 2006 current dollars. National Income and Product Account totals for annual total personal income is in current dollars.
- The increase in annual personal income is gradual from 2000 through 2040. The annual change in personal income becomes a decreasing percentage of the total until approximately 2033. This means that there will likely be increased drag on unemployment and a decline in average personal incomes for low and moderate-income citizens.
- Both the current economic crisis (Great Recession extended) and the Great Depression, were consequences of a peak and a decline in effective demand (housing and mortgages). Policies and projects developed by current and future presidencies best put primary emphasis on projects and policies that emphasize effective demand.
- Lingering unemployment will persist in the U.S. economy as long as a weak housing market continues. The prospect for a 10+ year drought in the U.S. housing market persists. This remains true as the number of homeowners who age and die will continue to increase, leaving used housing stock.

- Personal savings, as opposed to consumption, is undergoing a resurgence. Increase in personal savings has the effect of reducing disposable personal disposable income dollar for dollar.
- At this time, effective demand is best created by public and private investment in public goods, such as infrastructure, clean modes of transportation, clean forms of energy production, heating and cooling, education, and electronics.
- Those rewarded with contracts should be those who have developed or are in the process of developing practical energy alternatives that are highly efficient. Private individuals and firms should keep separate accounting records for each government contract. The government reinvestment should be returned over a 5 through 15 year period.
- Notes on the housing crisis.
  a. Some of the reasons for the housing crisis were;
    (1) Houses were sold to persons who did not have the income to sustain housing payments. This resulted in foreclosures, abandoned housing, and decline of neighborhoods.
    (2) In some areas of the U.S., too many houses were built. Supply exceeded demand.
    (3) The use of zero-down payment mortgages, adjustable rate mortgages (ARM), and an out-of-control mortgage making and investment process were elements of a mortgage investment and securitization process that eventually crashed.
    (4) Mortgages were made, bundled, securitized, and sold. Un-raveling securitized mortgages presents a continued problem. This is especially true when the lenders are taken to court.
    (5) Credit became too easy to obtain and then tightened after the housing bust.
  b. The reasons that housing market issues will not go away.
    (1) A large number of individuals aging and dying in the 2018–2040 period will leave behind used housing to be added to the existing housing stock.
    (2) There will be downward pressure on housing prices. Housing prices will decline further than their 2010 lows.
    (3) Demand for low income and middle income housing was saturated will remain saturated.
- There are six existing operational technologies that should be funded in public-private projects by federal loans repaid in a 5- through 15-year time period.
  - First, teams at three universities have produced operational methods for reducing emissions from coal-fired plants (MIT, Ohio University, and University of Arizona). A law requiring the adoption of these methods

by all coal-fired plants in the U.S. and its territories by a specified date should be passed. A program of government loans to private contractors working with coal-fired plants should accompany this effort. Vendors interested in developing and installation of pollution-free facilities should also be encouraged through the loan process.

- Second, geothermal energy should be developed through public-private partnerships from the slow volcanic energy available north of San Francisco into the states of Oregon and Washington. The power would be made available to major cities and other states. Existing technology would lend itself to such developments.
- Third, use of technology for wave-power energy generation has been developed. Also, tidal-power energy has been developed and is operational. Feasibility studies have been done for these types of energy generation. Studies indicate the U.S.-Pacific coast would be most amenable to wave energy and Maine and Alaska would be most amenable to tidal energy. Public-private partnerships should be funded to foster a rapid growth in these types of non-polluting energy resources.
- Solar energy has been developed that involves spraying a film over existing surfaces. This film uses both radiant energy and light to produce electrical power. Loans and tax write-offs should be developed to encourage adaptation of this type of highly efficient electrical production.
- The China Lake Naval Base in California has developed a partnership with a private company that has constructed a geothermal plant providing the base's energy needs as well as some for the grid. This results in the naval base receiving royalties. This example should be replicated on other federal property that lends itself to geothermal exploration.
- Programs modeled after the Roosevelt-era Civilian Conservation Corps (CCC), and the Work Progress Administration (WPA) should be instituted. In these instances, out-of-work youth and adults should apprentice rail-workers, steel workers, construction workers, electrical workers, alternative energy workers, etc. Those without a high school diploma would complete their high school studies while participating in the program.
- The United States Innovation Revolving Fund (USIRF) should be initiated as part of the U.S. Department of Energy to select, fund, and oversee the implementation of grants, loans, and innovations.
- A U.S. government-private partnership should be created for the production and sale of sun-gas. The Department of Energy's investment in the development of sun-gas should work to the purpose of lowering gas prices, lowering taxes, providing a clean fuel source, increasing government income, and sustaining a vital part of the private sector.

- The U.S. should modify its requirement that 100 percent of steel for alternative energy products be made in the U.S. A requirement of 80–90 percent domestically produced steel products could improve relationships with trading partners.
- The securitization of mortgages should be banned by a specified date. Existing mortgage securities would be allowed to mature or default. The Administration in power would assign an existing agency to enforce this.
- The immigration of students, Eastern and Asian professionals, and their families should be promoted by creating a special immigrant class. Adults in these families should be offered citizenship after remaining in the U.S. for three consecutive years and passing the necessary citizenship test.
- The U.S. government as well as private industry has ignored the non-polluting products developed by individuals in the New Energy Movement. It is time for the U.S. government and private industry to encourage the mass production of innovations that will reduce pollution and reduce the consumption of natural resources.
- It is recommended that quantum electromagnetic power be developed and be implemented for individual homes, power-generating plants, and for automobiles. This form of energy has the ability to solve the climate change problem as well as provide ready power for developing nations.

IMPLICATIONS FOR ECONOMIC THEORY

The role of monetary supply and effective demand needs to be revisited. A decline in effective demand results in increasing unemployment and a declining Gross Domestic Product (GDP). M_2 needs to be adjusted to the national economy's ability to generate aggregate demand.

- The research herein concludes that effective demand, personal income, personal consumption, and disposable personal income are generated by sex, age group, mean income, and numbers of groups defined this way with income.
- Of secondary importance, but still essential, is the money supply. It needs to be regulated in order to accommodate the expected levels of aggregate demand. To accommodate the possibility of growth, a 2 percent margin of monetary supply over aggregated demand is recommended. In case of contraction, reducing the money supply may be justified to avoid inflation.

- The major factors behind economic expansions and contractions are fluctuations in subgroup populations, and their variation in incomes of all types. The use of subgroup populations with incomes and mean subgroup incomes makes possible the calculation of total subgroup and total income for the income earning population.
- There are factors in the economy which make estimations difficult; increasing state and national debt, political differences over state and federal government budgets, moving jobs offshore, and poor management decisions at the state level.

M_2 is composed of two types of money; "central bank money" and "check-book money." Central bank money is loaned out by the central bank to banks in the banking system. The central bank money is paid back to a bank through the payment of a loan. In turn, the bank pays back the money to the central bank. The money in effect disappears. Check-book money originates with deposits by depositors. A fraction of the money is placed in the bank's reserves. The remainder of the money is loaned out. The individual(s) or businesses receiving the loans, deposit the money, creating more reserves (R) in banks and more money to loan out. The money multiplier (M) tells us how many times this goes on.

It is important to adjust the money supply (M_2) on the basis of variation in aggregate demand. Freidman recommended a 2 percent annual increase (.02) in money supply to accommodate growth. In a period of contraction, there is risk of inflation due to an excess of M_2 in the economy. For these reasons, the relationship between aggregate demand (AD), (M_2), and velocity (V) needs to be monitored closely.

Technical note: Lagged live births serve as a surrogate for an annual cohort of persons aged a particular number of years. Caution must be used to multiply the lagged live births by the survival rate for the given number of years in the lag to obtain the number surviving to that age.

CHAPTER 10

Deflation and Economic Crisis

At the time of publication of this book noteworthy events are taking place that confirm as well as question the analysis in this book. This statement references the sharp drop in oil prices in the U.S. As Harry Dent Jr. makes clear in his December 2014 "Boom & Bust" newsletter the continued decline of oil prices will lead to a fracking bust and a crash in the junk bond market that has supported the fracking industry and offered higher yields to investors.

Junk bond yields will increase and junk bond prices will decline. As this sector of debt goes bad the bond markets and the market in general will come under duress.

Dent (December 2014) maintains the Federal Reserve's quantitative easing has been accompanied by an increase in the value of junk bonds to 1.6 trillion dollars. While that has been occurring the interest rate on junk bonds has fallen to a record low of five percent in 2013 and 2014. Compared to the risk free 10-year treasury, the junk bonds were three percentage points higher.

The break-even price for fracking in the U.S. is currently between fifty-five dollars and eighty-five dollars per barrel. There is the expense of preparing rigs for production. Existing wells and stores will cause the supply to continue to expand in 2015. Thus, prices will continue to decline (Dent, December 2014). This is where the thesis set forth in this book comes into play. If demand for oil declines in 2015 until it reaches a low, it will occur at a time that the rate of personal income increase will be slowing (see Figure 10.1). The aging of the U.S. population, the lack of replacement personal income for those aging out of the workforce, the lack of a replacement population, and the unemployment in the fracking industry will be enough to result in a major economic depression.

FIGURE 10.1: Estimated Male and Female Total Personal Income, and Percent Change in Personal Income per Year

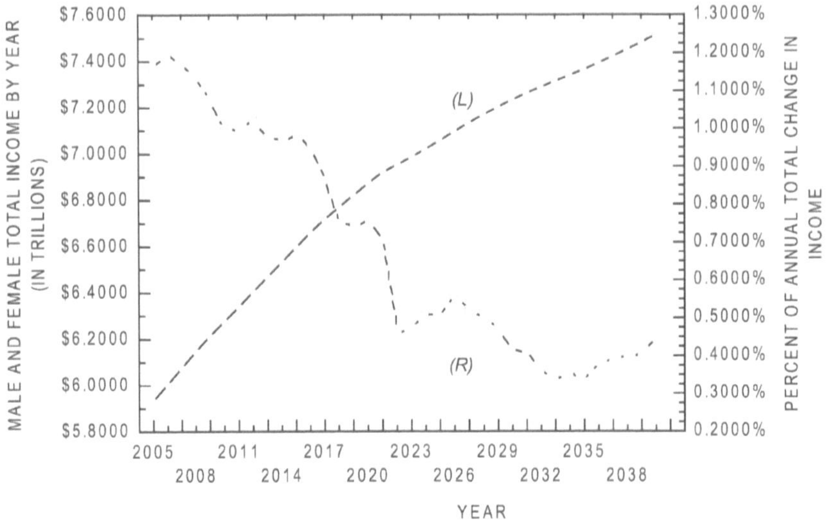

SOURCE: 2007 CURRENT POPULATION SURVEY (CPS), ASEC, AND ESTIMATED POPULATION BY AGE GROUP AND SEX (U.S. CENSUS BUREAU), 2005 - 2040

Central banks have been dealing with three deflationary trends. The Federal Reserve, using quantitative easing, has been attempting to deleverage national debt, deal with the aging of populations in developed nations, and confront deflation in commodity prices.

The policy options available to meet this depression are some of what has already been proposed. This will be a time of opportunity (if blame and name calling can be avoided). First, the price of gas in the U.S. should be allowed to vary between a level that is profitable for the producers but reasonable for consumers (not above two to two dollars twenty-five cents per gallon). Imports of foreign oil should have their price set at the same level or be refused entry into the U.S. Second, because the period of 2016 and beyond represents a period of low demand. This would be an excellent time to convert to sun-gas production and distribution nation-wide (see Chapter 9).

The author suggests a contrarian view. The deflation of oil prices makes available a consumer surplus for consumption and savings. If this reduction in gasoline prices (which is not certain) were accompanied by a nationwide hike in the minimum wage (which is happening in twenty-six states) the coming increase in personal income would occur at a more rapid rate, thus benefiting the economy of the U.S. If gas prices reach levels of about three dollars a gallon, the increase in consumption and savings will suffer. Part of the situation mentioned by Dent is a large part of U.S. domestic consumption is from domestic production. The degree to which foreign production replaces domestic production on the U.S. market determines in large part whether the domestic oil industry will be profitable. *Energy and Capital* (Angel Publishing House LLC, 2014) reports a suggestion by analysts of Deutsche Bank that if OPEC does not lower output, (and continues its price war against the West) then about nine percent of the U.S. marginal oil production would become uneconomical. If prices drop below eighty dollars a barrel the amount becomes forty percent.

All this points to a very uncertain future. Initially, looming in the economic and political horizon is the Trans Pacific Partnership (TPP). Its effect on employment and the U.S. economy is an unknown. If the TPP widens income inequality it will only build on existing trends. Second there is a new and cheaper method for extracting oil being developed and used in the U.S. This method, known as "Octopus" involves drilling a central-main pipe fed by a three-dimensional array of feeder pipes. This type of drilling makes possible digging fewer drill holes while covering a larger area of the underground. Third, the price per well is less than fracking as fewer wells are needed for the same or greater coverage. Last, what remains true is that the variation in oil prices [currently 48.12 dollars per barrel[1] (1/6/2015)] and the degree to which consumption is enhanced or retarded by oil prices will continue to be moderated through both mixed inflation and deflation of the price of goods and services caused by a mixed reaction of the private sector in passing price declines to consumers. This being true, all will be moderated through population subgroup characteristics and subgroup mean income. The slow growth of personal income remains very likely.

---

1. A barrel of oil is 42 gallons. Approximately 19 gallons go to gasoline, 12 gallons of diesel fuel, 4 gallons go to jet fuel, 6 gallons go to other products, and approximately 1 gallon is for other products and waste

References

American Incomes, Demographics of Who has Money. (2007). Sixth Edition, (New Strategist Publications, Inc., Ithaca, NY). This book takes data from the Current Population Survey, the Consumer Expenditure Survey, and the Federal Reserve Board's 2004 Survey of Consumer Finances.

Ataflion, Found in M. Stannett, "Assymetry of Economic Time Series Literature Survey 1825–1993", http:///www.dcs.shef.ac.uk/mps/assymetries, June 4–20, 2008.

Becker, Gary S. (1993*). Human Capital: A Theoretical and Empirical Analysis with Special Reference to Education*. Third Edition Originally Published in 1964. (National Bureau of Economic Research, University of Chicago Press, Chicago.)

Behrman, Found in M. Stannett, "Assymetry of Economic Time Series Literature Survey 1825–1993", http:///www.dcs.shef.ac.uk/mps/assymetries, June 4–20, 2008.

Beveridge, Found in M. Stannett, "Assymetry of Economic Time Series Literature Survey 1825–1993", http:///www.dcs.shef.ac.uk/mps/assymetries, June 4–20, 2008.

Blanchard, O. J. and S. Fischer: 1998, Lectures on Macroeconomics (The MIT Press, Cambridge, MA).

Bloom, D. and D. Canning. (2001) Cumulative Causality, Economic Growth and Economic Transition, in *Population Matters, Demographic Change, Economic Growth, and Poverty in the Developing World,* (eds) by N. Birdsall, A. C. Kelly, and S. W. Sinding, Oxford University Press, Cambridge, pp. 165–197.

Bouniation, Found in M. Stannett, "Assymetry of Economic Time Series Literature Survey 1825–1993", http:///www.dcs.shef.ac.uk/mps/assymetries, June 4–20, 2008.

Bureau of Census and Bureau of Labor Statistics, Current Population Survey, Annual Social and Economic Supplement, 1967–2000, http://www.census.gov/income, Accessed October, 2001.

Bureau of Labor Statistics, Department of Commerce, National Income and Product Accounts, http://www.bea.gov/national/nipaweb/TableView.asp?SelectedTable, accessed May 4, 2011.

Cagan, P. 1956. *The Monetary Dynamics of Hyperinflation* in Milton Friedman ed.: Studies in The Quantity Theory of Money (University of Chicago Press, Chicago), pp. 25–117.

Creamer, D. 1956. Personal Income During Business Cycles (National Bureau of Economic Research," (Committee for Economic Development, Supplementary Paper Economic Research, New York), (Princeton University Press, Princeton, NJ).

Denison, E. F. 1974. Accounting for United States Economic Growth 1929–1969 (Brookings Institution, Washington, D.C.).

Denison, E. F. 1962. "The Sources of Economic Growth in the United States and the Alternatives Before. (Committee for Economic Development, Supplementary Paper No. 13, New York.)

Dent, Harry S. Jr. (December, 2014). Boom & Bust/Flash Update. (Delray Publishing, Delray Beach, FL.)

Denton, Frank T, Byron G. Spencer. (1975) *Population and the Economy*, (Lexington Books, Lexington, MA.)

Diebold, F. X. and G. D. Rudebusch. 1999. Business Cycles, Durations, Dynamics, and Forecasting (Princeton University Press, Princeton, NJ).

Easterlin, R.E. 1965. 'Long Swings in U.S. Demographic and Economic Growth: Some Findings on the Historical Pattern,' *Demography*, pp. 490–507.

Feldstein M. (1991) Introduction, in (ed.) Martin Feldstein, The Risk of Economic Crisis, pp. 1–18, (National Bureau of Economic Research, University of Chicago Press, Chicago).

Ferber, R. 1953. A Study of Aggregate Consumption Functions, Technical Paper 8, (National Bureau of Economic Research, Inc., New York.)

The Financial Crisis Inquiry Commission (FCIC): January 2011, The Financial Crisis Inquiry Report (CFCR, 2011), (Government Printing Office, Washington, DC).

Fischer, I. 1928. The Money Illusion (Longmans, Green and Company, Toronto, Canada).

Fischer, I. 1911. The Purchasing Power of Money, Its Determination and Relation to Credit, Interest, and Crises. Revised Reprint 1925, (MacMillan, New York).

Friedman, M. and A. J. Schwarz: 1963, A Monetary History of the United States: 1867–1960 (National Bureau of Economic Research, Princeton University Press, Princeton, NJ).

Friedman, M. 1957. Theory of the Consumption Function (National Bureau of Economic Research, Princeton University Press, Princeton, NJ).

Friedman, M. 1956. '*The Quantity Theory of Money-A Restatement*' in Studies in the Quantity Theory of Money ed. Milton Friedman (University of Chicago Press, Chicago, IL) pp. 3–21.

Hobson, J.A., Found in M. Stannett, "Assymetry of Economic Time Series Literature Survey 1825–1993", http:///www.dcs.shef.ac.uk/mps/assymetries, June 4–20, 2008.

http://cdc.gov/nchs/data/nvsr/nvsr47/nvs47_13.pdf : Table 2. Number of survivors at single years of age, out of 100,000 born alive, by race and sex: United States, 1996, accessed August 14, 2007.

http://cdc.gov/nchs/data/nvsr/nvsr55/nvs55_01.pdf: Table 1. Live births, birth rates, and fertility rates, by race: United States, specified years 1940–55 and each year, 1960–2004, accessed August 14, 2007.
http://cdc.gov/nchs/data/statab//4941x.01.pdf: Table 1-1. Live Births, Birth Rates, and Fertility Rates, by Race: United States, 1909–1994, accessed August 14, 2007.
http://data.bls.gov/PDQ/servelet/SurveyOutputServelet: Major Sector and Costs Index, Manufacturing, Business, Non-farm Business, accessed October 9, 2007.
http://pubd3.census.gov/macro/032007/perinc/new01_010.htm: U.S. Census Bureau, Current Population Survey, 2007 Annual Social and Economic Supplement. Mean income for females by age, PINC-01- -Part 19. Accessed March 19, 2008.
http://pubd3.census.gov/macro/032007/perinc/new01_010.htm: U.S. Census Bureau, Current Population Survey, 2007 Annual Social and Economic Supplement. Mean income for males by age, PINC-01- -Part 10. Accessed March 19, 2008.
http://www.truthaboutcredit.org : Truth About Credit, accessed February 2, 2008.
Jaimovich H. and N. Siu (2007): "Sex and race as Related to Recessions," Federal Reserve Bank of St. Louis.
Kelly, A. C., and, R.M. Schmidt. (1995) Aggregate Population and Economic Growth Correlations: The Role of Components of Economic Change, *Demography*, 32, 4, pp. 542-555.
Keynes, John Maynard. (1937). (The Galton Lecture delivered before the Eugenics Society, February 16, 1937.) "Some Economic Consequences of a Declining Population", *Eugenics Review*, 29, no. 1: 13–17.
Keynes, J. M. (1936). The General Theory of Employment, Interest, and Money (Reprinted by Harcourt Brace Javonovich, N.Y., 1964).
Klein, J. J. 1956. *German Money and Prices, 1932-1944* in Milton Friedman ed.: Studies in the Quantity Theory of Money (University of Chicago Press, Chicago), pp. 121-159.
Koo, Richard C.: 2008, The Holy Grail of Macroeconomics, (John Wiley and Sons, Singapore).
Kuznets, S. (1979) *Growth, Population and Income Distribution*, Selected Essays, (W.W. Norton & Company, Inc., New York).
Kuznets, S. 1973. *Population, Capital, and Growth Selected Essays* (W.W. Norton & Company, New York).
Kuznets, S. 1966. *Modern Economic Growth, Rate, Structure, and Spread*, (Yale University Press, New Haven, CT).
Kuznets, S. (1965) *Economic Growth and Structure*, (W.W. Norton & Company, Inc., New York).
Kuznets, S. (1965b) *Toward a Theory of Economic Growth*, (W.W. Norton & Company, Inc., New York).
Kuznets, S. (1959) *Economic Growth*, (The Free Press of Glencoe, IL).
Lehrman, D. (2001) Why Micro Matters, in *Population Matters, Demographic Change, Economic Growth, and Poverty in the Developing World*, (eds) by N. Birdsall, A. C. Kelly, and S. W. Sinding, Oxford University Press, Cambridge, pp. 371-410.
Lescure, Found in M. Stannett, "Assymetry of Economic Time Series Literature Survey 1825–1993", http:///www.dcs.shef.ac.uk/mps/assymetries, June 4–20, 2008.

Malthus, Thomas Robert. (1993). *An Essay on the Principle of Population*. Originally published in 1798. Edited with an Introduction by Geoffrey Gilbert. (Oxford University Press, Oxford.)
May, Found in M. Stannett, "Assymetry of Economic Time Series Literature Survey 1825–1993", http:///www.dcs.shef.ac.uk/mps/assymetries, June 4–20, 2008.
Mitchell, W.C. 1913. Business Cycles (University of California Press, Berkeley, CA).
Mitchell, W.C. 1951. What Happens During Business Economic Cycles: A Progress Report, (National Bureau of Economic Research, Inc., Cambridge, The Riverside Press, Cambridge, MA).
Mitchell, W.C. 1961. Business Cycles: The Problem and Its Setting (National Bureau of Economic Research, New York). This is a reprint of original work done in 1927 and reprinted in 1936.
Modigliani, F. and R. Brumberg. 1954. "Utility analysis and the consumption function: an interpretation of cross-section data" in Kurihara, K. (ed.) Post Keynesian Economics, (Allen and Unwin, New Brunswick, NJ), pp. 338-436.
National Association of Realtors, 2010: Material supplied to FCIC.
National Bureau of Economic Research. 2002. National Bureau of Economic Research Dating Procedures, http://www.nber.org/cycles/recessions.html. Accesssed December 2009.
Posner, Richard A.: 2010, The Crisis of Capitalist Democracy, (Harvard University Press, Cambridge, MA).
Reddaway, Found in M. Stannett, "Assymetry of Economic Time Series Literature Survey 1825–1993", http:///www.dcs.shef.ac.uk/mps/assymetries, June 4–20, 2008.
Riley, J.: 2001. 'Silver Signals: Twenty-Five Years of Screening and Signaling', *Journal of Economic Literature* 39, pp. 438-478.
Rosenberg, Jerry M.: The Concise Encyclopedia of the Great Recession, 2007–2010.
Ruby, D.A. 2002. 'The Permanent Income Hypothesis of Consumption', http://www.digitaleconomist.com/pih_4020.html. Accessed June 2008.
Ruby, D. A. 2002. 'The Life-Cycle Hypothesis and the Rate of Time Preference', http://www.digitaleconomist.com/lch_4020.html. Accessed July 2008.
Schultz, Theodore W. (1963).*The Economic Value of Education*. (Columbia University Press, NY.)
Schultz, T. W. 1960. "Capital formation by education," *Journal of Political Economy,* 68, No. 6, 571–583.
Seater, J. J. 1998. 'Testing the Permanent-Income/Life-Cycle Hypothesis with Aggregate Data,' *acroeconomic Dynamics,* Vol. 2, 3. Pp. 401–425.
Shapiro, C. and J. Stiglitz. 1984. 'Equilibrium Unemployment as a Worker Discipline Device', *American Economic Review* 74, 433-444.
Shryock, H. L., J. S. Siegel and Associates. 1976. The Methods and Materials of Demography, Condensed Edition by Edward G. Stockwell, (Academic Press, NY).
Simon, Julian L. (1989). "On Aggregate Empirical Studies Relating Population Variables to Economic Development," *Population and Development Review,* 5, pp. 323-332

Solow, R. (1988), *Growth Theory, an Exposition.* (Contains both the Radcliffe Lectures 1969, and the Nobel Prize Lecture 1987), (Cambridge University Press, New York, London).

Solow, R. 1970. Growth Theory, An Exposition (Oxford University Press, New York).

Spiethoff, Found in M. Stannett, "Assymetry of Economic Time Series Literature Survey 1825–1993", http:///www.dcs.shef.ac.uk/mps/assymetries, June 4–20, 2008.

Staehle, H. 1937. 'Short-Period Variations in the Distribution of Incomes', *Review of Economic Statistics* 19, pp. 133–143.

Stannett, M. "Asymmetry of Economic Time Series Literature Survey 1825–1993", http:///www.dcs.shef.ac.uk/mps/asymmetries, Accessed June 4, 2008.

United States Census Bureau, Population Projections Branch. http://www.census.gov/population/www/projections/usinterimproj/usproj2000-2050.txt, accessed November 16, 2010.

U.S. Bureau of the Census, U.S. Department of Commerce: U.S. Population Estimates Age, Sex, White, Non-White, Resident. 1940–1969, Diskette May 2001.

U.S. Bureau of the Census, U.S. Department of Commerce: U.S. Population Estimates of the Resident Population Estimates by Age, Sex, Race, Resident. 1971–1979, Diskette. Accompanying related text for description of the data file, its origins and its contents. May 2001.

U.S. Bureau of the Census, U.S. Department of Commerce: U.S. Population Estimates by Age, Sex, Race, and Hispanic Origin, Resident. April 1, 1980–April 1, 1990, DSK.POP80/93-PE10. Diskette. See related text for description of the data file, its origins and its contents. May 2001.

U.S. Bureau of the Census, U.S. Department of Commerce: U.S. Population Estimates by Age, Sex, Race, and Hispanic Origin, Resident/Monthly. April 1, 1990–present, www.census.gov/population/www/disk/msdsk08d.html, Accessed October 2001, See related text for description of the data file, its origins and its contents.

U.S. Bureau of Census, U.S. Department of Commerce: (NP-D1-A) Annual Projections of the Resident Population by Age, Sex, Race, and Hispanic Origin, Middle Series, 1999–2100. http://www.census.gov/population/www/projections/natdet-1A.html, Accessed October 2001, See related text file for a description of the data file, its origins and its contents.

U.S. Department of Commerce, Economics and Statistics Administration, Bureau of Economic Analysis: *National Income and Product Accounts of the United States 1924–1994, Vol. 1–2,* April 1998.

U.S. Department of Commerce, Census Bureau, Housing and Household Economic Statistics Division, 2002. Telephone conversations with Ms. Shirley Smith and Mr. Robert Cleveland, March 4, 2002.

U.S. Department of Health and Human Services, Division of Vital Statistics: February 7, 2001, United States Life Tables, 1998, National Vital Statistics Report, Vol. 48, No. 18.

U.S. Immigration and Naturalization Service: INS Statistics page; "Statistics, Annual Statistical Reports"; http://www.ins.usdoj.gov/graphics/aboutins/statistics/index.htm, last modified 2/24/2000.

U.S. Life Tables 1998, National Vital Statistics Report, 2001, National Center for Health Statistics.

Whelpton, P. (1928) 'Population of the United States 1925–1975', *American Journal of Sociology*, 34, pp. 253–270.

Index

www.ingramcontent.com/pod-product-compliance
Ingram Content Group UK Ltd.
Pitfield, Milton Keynes, MK11 3LW, UK
UKHW041627031026
15587UKWH00001B/117

9 780761 866831